THE

POKER

THE
POKER
DIRECTORY

TREVOR SIPPETS

CHARTWELL
BOOKS, INC.

First published in the
United States in 2005 by
Chartwell Books, Inc.
A Division of Books Sales, Inc.
114 Northfield Avenue
Edison, New Jersey 08837
ISBN 0-7858-1941-X
Copyright © 2005
THE IVY PRESS LIMITED

This book was conceived,
designed, and produced by
THE IVY PRESS LIMITED
The Old Candlemakers, West Street,
Lewes, East Sussex, BN7 2NZ

Creative Director Peter Bridgewater

Publisher Sophie Collins

Editorial Director Jason Hook

Senior Project Editor Rebecca Saraceno

Design Manager Simon Goggin

Designer Jane Lanaway

Illustration Mark Jamieson

Photography APM Studios

Picture Research Vanessa Fletcher

Originated and printed in China

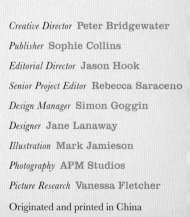

Contents

INTRODUCTION

I t may come as a surprise, given the range of leisure pursuits available to us via the technological wonders of the twenty-first century, that a card game with a history stretching back several hundred years continues to grow in popularity. That game is poker, the archetypal gambling game of skill, bluff, deception, and, sometimes, a little luck.

This fascinating card game still manages to hold the interest of people who want to socialize, play, and enjoy a little entertainment. Bring together a deck of cards, a group of people, and a little bit of imagination and you have the basic requirements for a few fulfilling hours of fun.

But you're competitive, right? So, throw in an element that stands to make winning worthwhile—cash, usually— and you have a betting game. Such is the appeal of poker. In fact, without the betting element, the game simply doesn't work. OK, it's possible to understand the game and theorize at length about strategy, technique and what constitutes a good hand. There will be a good deal of that in this book. But playing poker involves making decisions, and these decisions count because there is always a chance of winning—or losing—substantial amounts of money once you've exercised a choice to play or not. No amount of theory can

substitute for that experience because only you, as a player, can control how you react under proper playing conditions.

Each hand you play will be unique. It's true, of course, that the more often you play, the more you will encounter similar situations from game to game. That's how you build up experience. Yet, each time you have to make a betting decision in a hand of poker, there will be information hidden from you and disguised by your opponents. Play strongly enough to win a pot without showing your hand and you may never know all the factors that counted towards your triumph. No matter; rake in the chips. You can always ponder the merit of your play in that particular hand later. For now you'd be best advised to concentrate on the cards coming your way for the next hand. At its best and most enjoyable, poker is a high-tempo game involving many hands and, it follows, many chances to win or lose in quick succession. That's what makes it such a dynamic game.

Does that sound scary? Are you just a little intimidated? Well, if you're reading this, then you must at least want to know what the fuss is about. Since this book is aimed at the novice player, the focus will be to guide you through the basic rules of the game, explain the most popular variations of poker, and also offer a little bit of advice on betting and gaming strategy. Guidance on which hands to play and which hands to fold will feature, as will concepts behind successful bluffing. Armed with this information, you'll be ready to sit down and participate in a game. And since fear is often generated by ignorance, absorbing the knowledge contained within this book should help you to

BELOW
You can play poker just about anywhere, and you'll often get an audience.

take your place at the poker table with more confidence than before. Along the way you'll encounter some unfamiliar and colorful terms associated with the game. Don't worry. You'll be gently guided through the jungle of poker jargon that adds flavor to proceedings and acts as a shorthand for describing various plays or situations. Within a short while, you'll understand what is meant by slow playing a set before checkraising your opponents and crippling the deck. Before that, however, let's briefly consider where it all started and why poker remains at the forefront of the public consciousness.

BRIEF HISTORY

Most people regard poker as an American pastime, although the general consensus is that its origins are rooted in games played in Europe and Persia. It emanated from the ancient Middle East where it was known as *nas*, and the Italians of the fifteenth century enjoyed a poker-like game called *il frusso*. In Germany, recorded tales of the bluffing game *pochen* show it was still popular in the sixteenth century. A later variant emerged in France and this, in time, was exported to America via New Orleans and the steamboats of the Mississippi River. This game was called *poque* and it seems perfectly plausible that a corruption in the pronunciation of this word gave us poker.

So why is the game forever associated with America? In a word—Hollywood. While references to the game exist in cheap nineteenth-century novels, the fact is that poker regularly featured in Western movies and is an integral part of the mythology surrounding the Wild West. Seductive images of boisterous saloons populated by gunfighters resolving issues at the poker table, man-to-man, have helped secure the game's place in American culture.

BELOW
Wild Bill Hickcock was shot dead playing poker. He died holding two pair; two black Aces and two black 8s. A very bad beat!

Over the years, many variations of the game have been developed and players in the United States have been instrumental in popularizing the likes of Draw Poker, Five-Card Stud, Seven-Card Stud, Omaha High, and Texas Hold 'Em. The latter is arguably the most popular variation of all at present because it is the game most often played in poker tournaments around the world. It's the variation played at the World Series of Poker, another landmark in the history of the game.

The World Series was initiated in the early 1970s by Las Vegas casino owner Benny Binion. It was then a small event involving just a handful of legendary players, which nevertheless boosted poker's profile and helped re-define its appeal. Very quickly, the World Series grew sufficiently in stature to be

televised and that, in turn, has led to a proliferation of other tournaments around the world. Add to those the events that are staged purely for television audiences, often featuring celebrity players as well as notable pros, and some of the more lurid aspects of poker's reputation can be seen disappearing over the horizon. Poker is now enjoying a degree of respectability that it has been denied in the past.

The picture is completed by the development of the internet. Massive improvements in computer software have given rise to online casinos, enabling players of all abilities to play for fun or for money in a virtual world of almost limitless gambling possibilities.

The nature of the game remains the same, but poker's image has been cleaned up by these late-twentieth-century developments. Still, before the beginner is too dazzled by the opportunities on offer and the potential riches lying in wait, perhaps it's time to consider what you need to know in order to get started.

ABOVE
Poker now enjoys a degree of respectability, but it gained its fame from its representation as a seedy, late-night activity infused with danger in Hollywood movies.

POKER BASICS

This section is intended to provide an overview of the crucial factors that will help the novice player gain a foothold in understanding poker. The basic rules, regulation procedures, and the object of the game will all be covered. Some of the most common terms will also be explained as we proceed, and we'll look at some of the important factors to consider when playing in a home game. To help illustrate some of the concepts behind poker, we'll also look at a few sample hands and work through the mechanics of the most popular variations.

The extensive reach of American culture has ensured that poker terms have infiltrated the English language, to the extent that "Five-Card Draw" and "Five-Card Stud" are part of the everyday lexicon. Those who have never played will probably know that these are references to poker. A brief explanation of how to play these two versions will help you appreciate the anatomy of the game. A similar analysis of Texas Hold 'Em, probably the most popular poker variant of all, should provide a good foundation for understanding the exceptionally wide range of poker games, some of which will be covered in more detail later.

Before that however, perhaps we ought to consider the first crucial question—why play?

BELOW
Back in the old days, workers would play poker in their breaks, but the game could get rough.

WHY PLAY?

The reasons why human beings engage in sports and games are many and varied, yet it could be argued that they are all rooted in common desires. In nature, competition is rife and the competitive urges we all possess, stemming from our innate desire to survive and prosper, often drive us into situations of conflict. Thankfully, a few thousand years of civilization have enabled us to contrive forms of entertainment that generate the thrills of conflict and confrontation without us having to face any mortal risk.

BELOW
Playing for peanuts or high stakes, some guys just don't like losing. If the mood's intense, it could lead to mortal danger.

WIT, SKILL, AND COURAGE

Football and ice hockey, for example, involve pitting "armies" against each other in a battle for supremacy. A gentle round of golf can be viewed as one-to-one combat, with each player trying to prove himself superior in terms of skill. For the less physically active, chess endures as the classic board game in which each player marshals his forces in a bid to outwit his opponent and inflict defeat.

And then there's poker. Played at the highest level, it is a physically demanding game involving long sessions and intense periods of concentration. Poker is a game of wit, skill, and even courage. It is also a game for those who like to think, with each hand representing a puzzle that needs to be solved. The components forming the puzzle are you, the cards, your opponents, and the stakes for which you are playing. Gather together all the relevant information from these components before making a betting decision and you may find a solution that fattens your wallet.

ABOVE
Play well in poker and you stand a good chance of fattening your wallet.

Aside from the profit motive, poker offers plenty of scope for improving your psychological and emotional well-being. Play the game for peanuts rather than cash and what you are left with is a mechanism for satisfying your desire to win, and winning always feels good. But you cannot win every pot so the game also has the capacity for teaching players how to lose. Good players do it with grace, but good players also know how to avoid potentially costly battles in the first place. Remember, saving yourself from a heavy loss when holding a beatable hand is as important as maximizing your winnings when possessing the best hand.

Be prepared to examine yourself and your motives. Do you desperately want to win or merely enjoy a sociable game? If you like to win, what stakes appeal to you? And if you hate to lose, how will the strength of that emotion affect your play? Patience is a virtue in poker, as in life, and to expect every deal of the cards to present you with a winning opportunity is unrealistic. Wait for the moment when everything is in your favor and then pounce. That's the sort of play that generates respect at the card table.

So poker presents a great chance to be competitive, sociable, stimulated, inspired, and enriched, both emotionally and materially. Does that sound good? If so, you'll want to know what you need to start playing.

EQUIPMENT

he continued popularity of poker owes much to the minimal amount of equipment required to get a game going. Assuming you're already hooked on the idea of playing, you'll probably be looking to invite some friends around to test your skills.

THE DECK

The standard deck should have the regulation 13 cards in each of the four suits: clubs, diamonds, hearts, and spades. Some poker variations incorporate the use of a Joker or two but, for the moment, let's stick with the basic deck. Players may insist on a fresh deck at regular intervals throughout the session to ensure the game's integrity is not compromised. It's also worth suggesting that novelty decks be avoided. Anything that features images of movie stars or sports heroes will serve only to distract you from the task in hand. Beginners have enough to worry about when playing poker without trying to remember whether Robert De Niro is the King of diamonds. Or are you thinking *King of Comedy*? Whatever you're thinking, you've stopped focusing on the game for a moment and that can prove costly.

BELOW RIGHT
The four suits (clockwise from top left): hearts, clubs, diamonds, spades.

THE ESSENTIALS
◆

These are the essentials for any game so, if you want to play host, the minimum you will need is listed below.

☆ A standard deck of 52 cards

☆ Stake money and/or poker chips

☆ Some opponents willing to play

☆ A table at which to sit

☆ Sufficient seating for all players

Refreshments are an optional extra, bearing in mind that a session could last several hours, but how you organize them is up to you and your opponents.

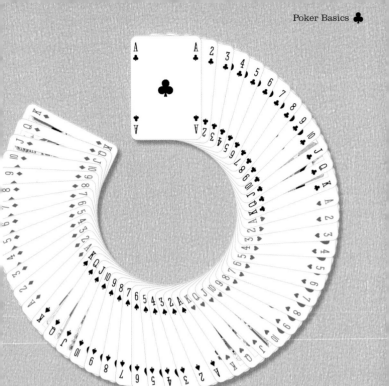

THE STAKES

As mentioned in the introduction, poker is a gambling game, which means you'll need some meaningful commodity with which to bet, usually cash. This is your "bankroll" or "sit-down money." If you visit a casino, you'll be supplied with gambling chips to the value of the stake money you deposit with the cashier. Hand over $100 and you'll receive chips representing that amount. These will be color coded, with the denomination indicated on each chip to help you make your bets. Having proper poker chips undoubtedly adds something extra to the experience of playing poker, and they also help to speed up the play. But if you and your friends only have a bunch of nickels and dimes in your pockets, or even tokens such as matchsticks, you can still get a game going.

The crucial thing to bear in mind when considering your bankroll is how much you are prepared to risk losing. If you'd think nothing of spending $50 on an evening out, why not use that as a guide to an evening's entertainment at the poker table? Whatever the case, set betting limits for the game to reflect the bankrolls held by each player. If you each have $50, it makes sense to set 50 cents as a minimum bet and $5 as the maximum.

ABOVE
The standard 52-card deck, featuring four suits of 13 cards each—clubs, hearts, spades, and diamonds.

THE PLAYERS

Poker is a game for between two and 12 players, with casinos usually looking to host between seven and ten participants per table, depending on the particular variation being played. For Texas Hold 'Em, 12 players can easily be accommodated with the cards available. But for that you'll need a big table.

RIGHT
"How about playing Jokers wild, do we have any takers?"

It is perfectly feasible for just two players to engage in a rewarding poker session, as was proved by a legendary game in 1949. That's when casino owner Benny Binion hosted a match between a couple of characters named Johnny Moss and Nick "the Greek" Dandalos. It lasted five months in all, with Dandalos finally calling a halt to proceedings once Moss had taken him for over $2 million. A game such as this is referred to as a "heads-up" contest. In tournaments, the last two players left at the table are said to be in a heads-up situation, but the term also applies to any two players contesting a pot after others have folded their hands.

Without wishing to be dogmatic about it, a game featuring between five and eight players offers a great chance to capture the dynamic essence of poker while providing a fair test of each player's ability. More than that and you run the risk of becoming involved in a slow game in which players can easily become distracted. This deprives you of the essential cut-and-thrust that is a feature of poker and eats into the time set aside for the session. Of course, if the distraction of chatting over a drink and debating who is going to win the big ball game seems natural to you, then that's fine, since poker is supposed to be fun and sociable, too.

Now, having considered the basic premise of the game and the equipment required to play, it's time to take a look at a few rules.

THE TABLE AND CHAIRS

Human beings are pretty resourceful creatures so there's
not too much point dwelling on the standard of table
and seating available for a game. A custom-made table
complete with a green baize covering and a dozen
matching chairs is great, but not essential. Casinos have
such round or possibly kidney-shaped tables at which to
play but, away from the glamor of the gaming room,
real card players take advantage of whatever's available.
Just make sure that everyone is able to sit in comfort, and
there's room for the cards and the chips.

BASIC RULES

Then let us assume you have gathered together all the equipment you need for a game. You and your buddies now have to decide which poker variation to play. There are plenty to choose from but, for the moment, let's concentrate on the common procedures that apply to poker in general.

THE OBJECT OF THE GAME

Since poker is a gambling game, the main objective is to win your opponents' money, most usually represented in the form of gaming chips. To do this you must win pots, the pot being the sum total of chips wagered by all participants during the playing of each individual hand. And a hand is the term used to describe each game, customarily lasting just a few minutes, that takes place during a poker session. At the same time, a hand is also the term that describes the cards dealt to each player during the game.

But how do you win a pot? Well, there are two ways of reaching a decision in each hand of poker. Either a player wins by making a bet that no other player is prepared to match, allowing him to rake in the chips without revealing his hand. Or, in the event of two or more players matching stakes through to the conclusion of the hand, those contesting the pot reveal their hands in what is called the "showdown." At this stage, the player possessing the best hand wins. Some poker variations incorporate the use of more than five cards in a hand—Seven-Card Stud and Omaha for example—but remember, only the best five cards will count in the final reckoning.

WINNING POTS

Bear in mind that winning a lot of pots does not always mean winning the most money. The betting aspect of poker ensures that there is always something to play for in each hand, but be wary of allowing your competitive instincts to control your game. On a majority of occasions you can expect to fold your hand early and say "adios" to a few of your chips. But those occasions need not hurt if you are prudent with your betting decisions. Winning a few big pots at crucial moments is likely to prove more profitable in the long run.

WHO WINS?

◆

At the showdown, it is possible that two or more players will have a hand of the same rank. Under normal circumstances, the pot would be split equally between them. The important thing to remember is that the best five-card hand wins. To win without revealing your hand, you must make a bet that is not matched by any of your opponents. There are two occasions when you might achieve this. When you have a strong hand and you're happy to advertise it as such with a big bet. Or when you have a weak hand that you are deliberately misrepresenting as strong to intimidate your opponents. And that, of course, is bluffing.

THE DEAL

To start a game, someone must deal the cards. But how do you decide who deals first? In a casino or club, of course, a professional dealer is employed to help run the game smoothly and fairly. This is a crucial part of the dealer's responsibilities and, in a home game, the dealer monitors play to ensure everyone observes the rules.

Usually, players cut for the deal with the lowest card taking the honor. For the cut, Aces are high cards, and 2s are the lowest. If two or more players cut the same value card, then they repeat the procedure until a dealer is decided.

BELOW
Cut the cards to decide who deals first. The lowest card takes the honor.

I'll deal and I promise I won't make any fast moves. How does that sound to you, honey?

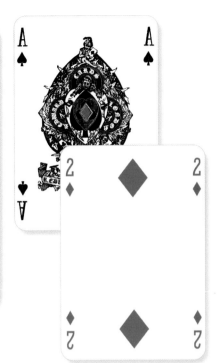

THE DEALER BUTTON

◆

The dealer button, or "buck," is used in clubs and casinos to indicate who has the status of dealer in each hand. Since a professional dealer will be distributing the cards, the button moves one place to the left after each hand to make it clear who receives the first card and who, in most cases, will make the first bet. The phrase "passing the buck" is derived from this act of passing the dealer button clockwise around the table as the game progresses.

DEALER

The dealer must shuffle the cards before each hand, taking care not to expose any cards in the deck. Having shuffled, it is customary for the dealer to pass the deck to the player on his right so that the cards may be cut. To cut, simply pick up the top half of the deck and place it face down on the table. Then place the bottom half of the deck on top of the other cards. This helps eliminate cheating.

Next, the dealer must ensure that those players required to "ante-up" in advance place their chips in the pot. The ante is a compulsory bet, but the number of players required to bet before receiving a card varies depending on the game that is being played.

Beginning with the player on his immediate left, the dealer then distributes the cards one at a time from the top of the deck to each player in turn, working clockwise around the table, until each player has the required number of cards for the variation being played. In Draw, each player receives five cards face down, but in Five-Card Stud, players start with just two cards—the first face down, and the second face up.

In most variations, the player can look at his own concealed cards, but these are of course kept hidden from his opponents.

THE BETTING

As poker is a gambling game, betting is an integral part. Each variation has a specific number of betting rounds in each hand and the pattern of betting may also vary, but the choices available to you, whatever game you play, are the same. To illustrate the basics, let's picture a simple game of low-stakes Draw poker featuring five players: Wild Bill, Doc, Annie, Calamity, and Jesse.

Before the cards are dealt, the dealer should ensure that sufficient antes are in the pot. Ordinarily, each player in a game of Draw should ante-up with a nominal bet and, in this example, we'll make it a quarter each to play. That puts $1.25 in the pot and immediately generates a bit of interest around the table. Once five cards are dealt face down to each player, they all look at their respective hands before the betting begins for real.

BELOW
The cards shown here are Doc's opening hand.

❖ LET'S LOOK AT THE TABLE ❖

Jesse is dealing so the player to his left—Wild Bill—has to make the first decision at the start of this betting round and he has three options: to check, to bet, or to fold. If he checks, he is deferring a decision to bet at this stage. This is only an option if no other player in the round has already made a bet and, since player one is acting first, obviously this is the case. Wild Bill checks.

Now the "action" moves to Doc in seat two. As Wild Bill checked, Doc also has this option available to him, or he can fold. However, he likes his hand and decides to bet 50 cents. For Annie in seat three, checking is not permitted since a bet has been made. To stay in the game, she must make a bet of at least 50 cents and "call" Doc's bet. But Annie also has two other options. She can "raise" Doc by calling his bet of 50 cents and then adding more to the pot, or she can "fold" (or pass) her hand, thus taking no further part in the game. If she folds, she forfeits her ante of a quarter.

Annie isn't impressed by Doc's bet so she decides to raise him. She announces "raise" and puts $1 into the pot. This represents 50 cents to call Doc's bet, and another 50 cents to make the raise. Most games will have specified levels of betting as the rounds progress but, for the moment, remember that any raise should be at least equal to the previous bet. In this case, Annie makes the minimum raise possible.

Now it is Calamity's turn. She cannot check, of course, and must at least call $1 to match Annie's bet and continue in the game. Deciding the stakes are too high and her hand too weak, Calamity folds and puts her cards in the "muck," this being the term for the pile of discarded cards. Now the action is on Jesse, the dealer, in seat five.

The dealer position is useful because of the advantage of betting last in the round. Jesse has more information to go on, for instance, than Wild Bill who checked in seat one. Perhaps that was a sign of weakness on Wild Bill's part, but Doc liked his hand enough to bet and Annie quickly raised him to increase the pressure on her opponents. Jesse calls Annie's bet of $1 meaning that the action is back on Wild Bill who, by checking earlier, delayed his decision.

Wild Bill knows that he must now bet at least a dollar to continue in the game, but his hand is weak, as Jesse suspected, and he folds. Doc in seat two, remember, made the initial bet of 50 cents and now has to match the bets of $1 from Annie and Jesse to stay alive. He could raise again if he wishes, but he adds another 50 cents to the pot and announces "call," to conclude the betting for this round.

❖ LET'S LOOK AT THE TABLE ❖

RIGHT
Annie discards two cards in the hope of something better to come.

Ok cowboy, I'll have another two cards over here.

Now the three players who have matched stakes of $1 each to stay in the game are ready for the "draw," which gives Draw poker its name. Beginning on the dealer's left, each player in turn discards any cards from their hand that they no longer wish to play, from a minimum of no cards at all to a maximum of all five.

Since Wild Bill is out of this particular hand, Doc draws first and decides to discard three cards. The dealer ensures these cards are in the muck and then deals Doc the top three cards from the deck to restore his hand to five cards. Annie wants to replace two cards from her hand, so she follows the same procedure by discarding the unwanted cards, while Jesse deals her two replacements from the top of the deck. Finally Jesse himself makes his decision and he opts to stay put with his original five-card hand. By drawing no replacement cards he is said to be playing a "pat hand," often a sign of strength. Alternatively, Jesse could be bluffing by trying to convey the impression of a strong hand.

Doc, you sure are one hell of a checkraiser.

LEFT
Doc checks and later raises. Maybe he is bluffing... maybe.

There is currently $4.25 in the pot, comprising the $1.25 in antes from all players and $1 each from Doc, Annie and Jesse. Now the second and final betting round begins with Doc first to act. The three cards he drew don't appear to have helped as Doc checks, maybe revealing that he doesn't have a strong hand. Maybe. Annie, who drew two cards, could check too if she wanted, since no money has yet been staked in this round. However, she bets $1 and pressurizes her opponents, who must now bet or fold.

Jesse, playing a pat hand remember, matches Annie's dollar and raises another dollar for good measure before the action passes back to Doc, who checked earlier. Doc faces a bet of $2 just to call now, but he decides to announce a raise. He first matches Jesse's $2 bet and then raises by another dollar, this being the value of the previous raise by Jesse. This is known as "checkraising" since Doc checked at his first betting opportunity only to bet strongly with another raise when the action came back around to him.

Following Doc's checkraise, Annie now has to bet at least $2 to call but, although she has already contributed $2.25 to the pot (a quarter for the ante, $1 in the first betting round and another $1 in this round), she believes his hand is stronger and decides to fold now and cut her losses. Another factor in her decision is that Jesse, who is sat to her left waiting his turn again, is playing with a pat hand *and* raised her bet a moment ago. If she folds, is he likely to relinquish his hand and let Doc take the money uncontested? Probably not, so Annie knows that she is likely to be competing against two strong hands and thinks that discretion is the better part of valor on this occasion. Of course, Doc and Jesse could both be bluffing outrageously and she may have just folded a winner. But it's her money, her decision, and she knows a better opportunity may be along soon. So the action returns to Jesse.

If Jesse folds now, Doc can claim the pot without revealing his cards. If he calls for the extra $1 by which Doc raised, then the betting ends and both players reveal their hands in a "showdown," with the best hand winning the pot. Alternatively, he can re-raise Doc by calling the $1 and betting at least $1 more to up the stakes again. The general rule in most poker games is that raises should be limited to three or four per betting round, except when there are just two players still contesting the pot, at which point there is no limit on the number of raises and re-raises.

❖ LET'S LOOK AT THE TABLE ❖

JESSE'S HAND

Jesse actually has an Ace-high flush in diamonds in his hand, meaning that he has five assorted diamonds, including the Ace, without the cards combining in a sequence to make up a royal flush. It's pretty good but not unbeatable, so he calls the $1 that Doc raised and concludes the betting for the entire hand. Both Doc and Jesse simultaneously place their cards face up on the table for the showdown, at which point Doc reveals a full house of 8s over 5s, meaning three 8s complemented by a pair of 5s, making him the winner. A full house is ranked higher than a flush so Doc scoops the pot and adds the total stake of $11.25 to his stack. The cards are then passed to Jesse's left where Wild Bill prepares to deal the next hand.

This example conveys the basics of poker betting and touches on some of the strategic thinking that each player must employ, not just to win a pot, but also to avoid losing chips unnecessarily.

DOC'S
WINNING HAND

CHECKRAISING

◆

Poker is a game in which
players try to outwit and
deceive each other, and
employing checkraising is a
legitimate way to keep your
opponents on their toes.
However, not everyone
approves of such a sneaky
move, so check the rules of
the club or home game at
which you're playing just
to make sure it's permitted.
Personally, I think checkraising
is fine because it adds another
exciting dimension to the
game. However, some
players consider it
almost dishonorable.

DETERMINING THE RESULT

The previous sections show you how a winner is determined. Now let's look in more detail at exactly what takes place. As well as rules, there's also poker etiquette to follow at the poker table, which relates specifically to the resolution of each hand.

First, just to recap, there are two ways of winning a pot. Either you make a bet that is not matched by your opponents, who all fold, leaving you to rake in the chips. Or the game is concluded with a showdown, meaning that the players who have matched stakes to the conclusion of all betting rounds must reveal their hands, with the strongest hand claiming the spoils.

In the latter instance, all involved should reveal their hands simultaneously in full view of all other players. This ensures that any winning claim can be verified to everybody's satisfaction before the chips are added to the winner's stack. Sometimes the player making the final calling bet to provoke the showdown—Wild Bill, perhaps—may announce that he is "seeing" the previous bet to indicate a call. This is common, but it does not mean that the player being called—Annie, let's say—must reveal her hand *before* her adversary shows his cards. If she does so and the caller can see he is beaten, he may muck his cards without revealing them to the rest of the players, which is poor practice. Of course, the reason players do it is that they do not want to give away information that might be useful to their opponents. In this case, Wild Bill could conceal the type of hand he was prepared to support right through to the showdown. Anyhow, there's always the possibility that in denying others the chance to see his cards, Wild Bill may unwittingly muck a winning hand. Do you want that to happen to you?

Concealing information is at the hub of the next point when it comes to winning without showing your hand. If you have bet enough to intimidate all your opponents into folding, you can muck your hand with all the others and rake in the chips. Of course, everyone will want to know what cards you held to see if you were bluffing or not. The rule is clear—you are not compelled to reveal your cards. "Pay to play, or no way," should be the guiding principle on this issue.

However, there are times when players are quite happy to reveal their cards in this situation, whether showing a good hand or a complete bluff. If you do it, and there are legitimate tactical reasons for doing so, then the general principle is "show one, show all," which means everyone at the table sees the cards.

ABOVE
**A big bet can often
intimidate even the meanest-
looking opponent.**

SOME POINTERS ON HOME GAMES

Casinos and clubs have their own regulations to ensure an efficient and fairly run poker game and players will be expected to observe the formal conventions. Such regulations are not necessarily standardized, and it is up to you to take responsibility for your conduct and familiarize yourself with the relevant protocols.

But what about home games? Whether it is your turn to play host or you are invited to an established card school for the first time, make sure you clarify potentially contentious issues. It is always worth having the rules recorded on paper to avoid disputes over some of the following eventualities.

For a start, when is the game scheduled to begin and end? Is there a minimum acceptable period for someone to play before quitting the game? If you have to leave early, tell the other players before you sit down. To understand why, just picture yourself well ahead after an hour and then announcing that you must go, preventing the others from winning some of their money back. How popular do you think you'd be?

BELOW
Home games need clearly-defined rules to avoid potential disputes between players.

Rule 537: any player who has los big pot can contemp his folly at any ti

WHICH GAME?

Then there is the decision on which game to play. One popular option is to abide by the "dealer's choice," meaning that the dealer nominates the variant to be played. This presents the chance to engage in a wide range of poker games, allowing players to broaden their knowledge and skills. On the other hand, if most players at the table are fairly new to poker, half the session could be spent trying to explain the specific rules of yet another new variation. And that's before you consider whether to use wild cards, as is the case with a poker game such as Baseball.

PLAYING WITH WILD CARDS

Using wild cards to liven up a game is common as it offers the potential for more winning opportunities because you can count the nominated wild card as any value card necessary to improve a hand. It may be decided, for instance, that "deuces are wild," so the four 2s in the deck can be counted as any card of a higher value. Again, be clear on the home game rules. For example, does a royal flush consisting of an Ace, King, and Jack of diamonds, plus any pair of 2s substituting for the Queen and the 10 of diamonds, count as the equal of a "natural" royal flush, or is it inferior? Also, take into account that a hand will probably need to be stronger than normal to merit support in a wild-card game.

DIVIDING SPLIT POTS

Another aspect to consider is the dividing of split pots when players showdown hands of equal value. How are these to be divided and what happens to any odd chips left over after each player has claimed their share? In high/low games, (*see page 112*, for example), how should players indicate which element they are attempting to win? One way is for players to declare their intention by concealing chips in their hand—one chip for low, two chips for high, and three chips for both halves of the pot. The players then reveal the chips in their hand prior to the showdown so that everyone knows where they stand.

BELOW
A successful poker game means playing by the rules.

Hey, let's make sure we all know exactly where we stand.

MORE BETTING ETIQUETTE

Other pointers on betting etiquette relate to chip handling. "Splashing the pot" by dumping your chips in among the others already staked can lead to confusion. Have you put in too much, or not enough? You can avoid being accused of short-changing the pot simply by making clear bets and announcing exactly what you intend to do. Ordinarily, players should each make a bet by placing the required number of chips in a neat stack just in front of them. That way everyone can see what has been staked and who is entitled to continue in any particular hand.

Try not to bet out of turn. If you make a big raise before the player to your right has decided what to do, that may be the cue for him to fold his hand instead of swelling the pot by a few bucks with a modest bet. If your hand is a guaranteed winner, you'll have just reduced the prize on offer, and that's no way to make your poker profitable.

As a rule, players should keep their cards face down in clear view of their opponents to indicate their continued participation in a hand. Folded hands should be put in the muck. Each player's chip stack or bankroll should also be clearly visible to all, and if an opponent wants to know how much you have left before committing himself to a bet, let him know as this is perfectly acceptable.

MAKE UP YOUR MIND!

One final point to consider concerns time. How much time is to be allowed for a player to make a decision? Poker is supposed to be a quick and dynamic game but there will be occasions when a player faces an important, and potentially expensive, betting decision. Have a ruling in place to cover this situation. For guidance, why not adopt the practice of allowing a player two minutes for a decision from the moment an opponent queries whether he is betting or folding. Putting him "on the clock" when he has already spent a few minutes in thought encourages decisive play and keeps the game flowing.

BUY-INS AND BANKROLLS
◆

Most tournaments feature an entry fee called a "buy-in," typically ranging from $100 up to $10,000 depending on the size and prestige of the event. For this, each player starts the game with the same amount of chips. Since the object of tournament play is to produce one overall winner, once you've lost your chips, you're out. This is typical of "freeze-out" events.

However, in some "re-buy" tournaments, if you've lost your bankroll it is permissible to obtain more chips by paying another entry fee, though this facility is usually offered during the first hour or two of play only. For your home game, decide whether you want to apply a freeze-out or re-buy option and, if permitting a re-buy, insist it is done between hands. Buying more chips to provide extra ammunition during the playing of a hand is generally unacceptable behavior.

RANKING OF HANDS

The card combinations set out over the next few pages illustrate the basic ranking of poker hands. This section will also provide some more detail on the rankings and their relative strengths. With over two and a half million different five-card combinations available in a standard 52-card deck, the hands are ranked according to the likelihood of them appearing. The rarest hand is ranked highest and the most probable combination is lowest. All four suits in poker are of equal value and Aces can count high or low.

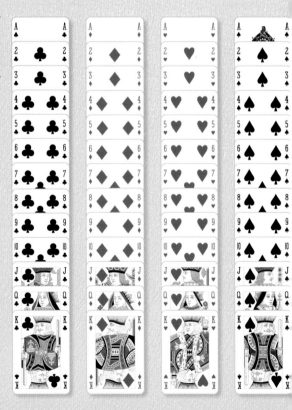

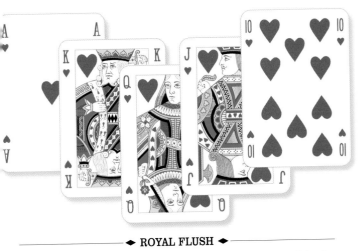

◆ ROYAL FLUSH ◆

The royal flush is the top ranking hand in poker and consists of the five highest cards in any one of the four suits. For example, the Ace, King, Queen, Jack, and 10 (A, K, Q, J & 10) of hearts is a royal flush, or royal straight flush if you prefer. There are, of course, only four possible royal flush combinations available.

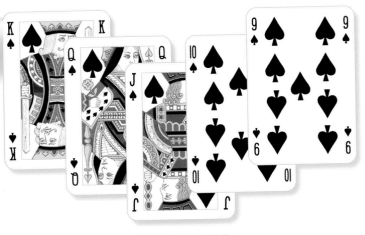

◆ STRAIGHT FLUSH ◆

The second-best hand in poker is a straight flush, consisting of five cards of the same suit in sequential order. There are 36 possible straight flush combinations, the highest being K, Q, J, 10, and 9 in any of the four suits. The lowest would comprise the 5, 4, 3, 2, and Ace. The highest card in a straight flush determines the winner in the event of two players having a similar hand. For example, a J, 10, 9, 8, and 7 of spades beats a 10, 9, 8, 7 and 6 of diamonds.

◆ FOUR OF A KIND ◆

As it suggests, four cards of the same value plus an odd card. For example, 10 of clubs, 10 of diamonds, 10 of hearts, 10 of spades, plus a 3 of clubs.

◆ FULL HOUSE ◆

A full house comprises three cards of one value combined with two of another. The highest full house is A, A, A, K, K and the lowest 2, 2, 2, 3, 3, with the strength of the hand dictated by the three cards of the same value. For instance, Q, Q, Q, 2, 2 beats J, J, J, A, A since the supporting pair is irrelevant in determining the better hand.

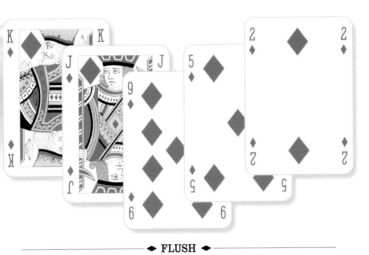

♦ FLUSH ♦

A flush is five cards of the same suit that are not in sequence. For example K, J, 9, 5, 2 of diamonds (a King-high flush) or 9, 8, 6, 4, 3 of spades (a 9-high flush). The high card of the flush dictates its value, so an Ace-high flush beats a King-high flush, and a 10-high flush beats a 9-high flush. If two players both hold flushes with the same value high card, then the value of the second-highest card comes into play. If they are equal in value, then the third-ranked card is decisive, and so on down to the fifth card. So Q, J, 7, 6, 3 of spades beats Q, J, 7, 5, 4 of diamonds, and A, K, 9, 3, 2 of hearts beats A, K, 8, 7, 6 of clubs.

I think I can feel a hot flush coming on...

◆ STRAIGHT (OR RUN) ◆

A sequence of five cards in a mixture of suits, for example Q of hearts, J of spades, 10 of clubs, 9 of hearts, and 8 of hearts. The Ace can count high or low so A of diamonds, K of clubs, Q of diamonds, J of spades, and 10 of clubs would be a top-ranked Ace-high straight, while 5 of hearts, 4 of spades, 3 of spades, 2 of hearts, and A of clubs would be a lowly 5-high straight.

◆ THREE OF A KIND ◆

Simply three cards of the same rank plus two odd cards, for instance, K of diamonds, K of hearts, and K of spades, plus J of hearts and 8 of clubs. Another example is 10 of clubs, 10 of hearts, 10 of spades, plus A of diamonds, and 5 of spades.

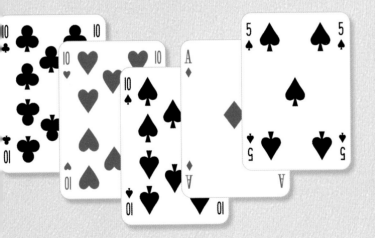

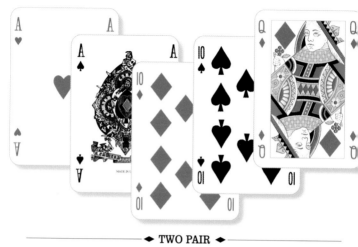

◆ TWO PAIR ◆

A common hand in poker comprising two cards of one value, two cards of another value, and an odd card called the "kicker." For example A of hearts, A of spades, 10 of diamonds, 10 of spades, plus a Q of diamonds. The highest pair in the hand is decisive so A, A, 2, 2, 5 will beat K, K, Q, Q, J. If competing hands hold the same high pair then the second pair comes into play, with 10, 10, 9, 9, 6 superior to 10, 10, 5, 5, A. If players hold two pairs of identical value, then the kicker is decisive.

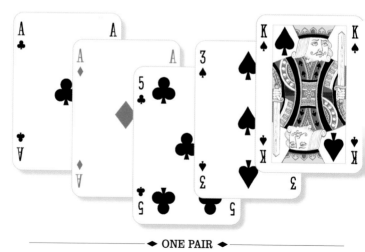

◆ ONE PAIR ◆

Two cards of the same value plus any three odd cards. The value of the pair determines the strength of the hand, but if two players hold the same value pair, then the remaining cards come into play. A, A, K, 5, 3 beats A, A, Q, J, 10, and Q, Q, K, 9, 5 beats Q, Q, K, 8, 6.

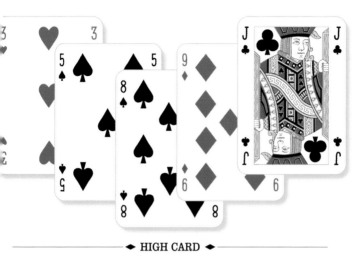

◆ HIGH CARD ◆

A hand containing five assorted cards without even a pair. Again, competing hands are ranked according to their highest card, then the second-highest, and so on down to the fifth card.

WILD CARDS
◆

It is worth bearing in mind that if you play wild-card games then an additional hand of "five of a kind" can come into play. This normally ranks below a royal flush and above a straight flush, but it's best to check the house rules on this before you sit down. Similarly, be clear on whether a royal flush incorporating wild cards is equal or inferior to a "natural" royal flush.

RIGHT
If you are playing the game with deuces as wild, then this hand becomes five of a kind.

DRAW POKER

This section is intended to help beginners understand the anatomy of poker, using examples from three popular variants. Working through sample hands of Five-Card Draw, Five-Card Stud, and Texas Hold 'Em will help you appreciate the reasoning behind decisions made at the poker table. Absorbing some of the lessons here will prepare you for a in-depth look at these and other popular poker variants discussed later in the book.

THE DEAL

The basic pattern of play in Draw poker was explained in the earlier section on betting (*see pages 24–31*) so you now have an idea of how the game works. For ease of reference, we'll rejoin our five players at the table—Wild Bill, Doc, Annie, Calamity, and Jesse—to witness how the game is progressing. In this instance, the players have agreed to play a "fixed limit" game of $1–$2, meaning that the first round of betting, after the deal, is limited to bets of $1 denominations, and the second round requires that bets are made in $2 increments. All of the players are required to put in their ante, which is set at 50 cents apiece so, with the pot worth $2.50, Wild Bill has the honor and deals the players their five cards each.

Doc has a pair of Kings (Ks) and an Ace (A), and is also looking at three hearts. Since he has the top two hearts already, he is contemplating a draw of two cards to make an Ace-high flush. But he could retain the pair of Ks and hope to improve his hand to four of a kind or a full house. Annie also has a pair but her 10s are inferior to Doc's Ks, though she cannot know that at the moment since, obviously, nobody knows what cards their opponents are holding.

Hey, buddy, if you're thinking about going for Draw, you'd better be good.

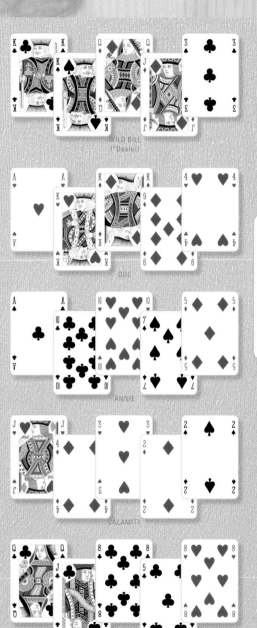

Calamity has been dealt a pair of 2s and, with a 3 and a 4 in her hand, has the chance of drawing a low straight should she decide to discard the Jack (J) and a 2. An A and a 5, or a 5 and a 6 would be required for this to happen. Jesse's pair of 8s is not strong but, with a 4 of clubs in his hand, he has a realistic chance of hitting a flush if he chooses to discard the 8 of hearts. Finally, Wild Bill holds a pair of Ks, just like Doc, and he has a chance of hitting an A and a 10, or a 10 and a 9 to make a straight, should he decide to hold on to either King (K), the Queen (Q) and the Jack (J).

THE FIRST BETTING ROUND

Before the draw there is a betting round and Doc acts first. He is in "early position" and checks, hoping to obtain more information from his opponents' decisions to help him gauge the strength of his pair of Ks. Annie, with a lower pair, checks as well, as does Calamity who is not prepared to bet in "mid-position" with her small pair of 2s. With a low "starting hand," she believes her opportunity to win is poor, but she may be prepared to stay in the game provided any betting is for low stakes. Indeed, if everyone checks before the draw stage, she may be able to improve her hand considerably without having paid for the privilege.

Jesse thinks that trying to obtain a flush in clubs represents the best opportunity to improve his hand and bets $1 on the strength of this. He has four clubs and knows that there are nine others among the remaining 47 cards in the deck. The odds against him drawing a club are therefore slightly over 4 to 1, with nine cards working for him and 38 against. Wild Bill acts last and he calls Jesse's bet of $1. Doc now feels that his pair of Ks may be worth playing so he calls for a $1, as does Annie. Calamity decides that her pair of 2s is too weak and she folds. There is a total of $6.50 in the pot.

AFTER THE DRAW

Now we see the player's hand after the draw. Annie has the best hand with two pair, 10 and 9.

THE DRAW

The next stage of the game is the draw when plenty of information is on offer. Doc discards two cards, keeping the pair of Ks and the A, but he receives the 7 of clubs and 4 of spades, so his hand has not improved.

Annie exchanges three cards, perhaps highlighting to her opponents that she retains a pair in her hand, but she picks up another pair with two 9s, giving her a reasonable hand of two pair. Calamity folded so Jesse draws next and he exchanges one card, discarding the 8 of hearts and receiving the A of spades. In retaining four of his initial cards, Jesse implies a degree of strength in his hand. The others may calculate that he is seeking a card to make a flush or a straight, but he could be concealing four of a kind, three of a kind, or two pairs. However, though the others don't know it yet, his attempt to make a flush has failed. Wild Bill announces that he is drawing three cards but, like Doc, his hand is slightly weakened when he receives 10, 7, and 2.

THE FINAL BETTING ROUND

Now the final betting round begins and, with limits fixed at $1–$2, the minimum bet is now $2. Doc figures that Annie and Wild Bill were both holding a pair before the draw and he is more worried about Jesse. Nevertheless, he bets $2. Annie knows Doc is likely to gamble whatever cards he holds but she is a bit concerned that, in retaining three of his starting cards, he may have at least three of a kind, and that would beat her two pair. She is also wary of Jesse but wants to stay alive in the hand so she calls Doc's $2 bet, believing that her cards are worth backing with a small stake.

Jesse, who only has A high, knows that any pair beats him and he is certain that someone will have at least a pair. If he calls the $2 and Wild Bill either folds or calls, the showdown will reveal his hand to be a loser. To win from here he has to raise the pot and try to convince the others that he has, indeed, drawn the flush or straight that they probably suspect he was attempting. But successful poker is about minimizing losses as well as maximizing winning opportunities so Jesse folds.

For Wild Bill, the situation is similar to Jesse's in that he believes his hand will be beaten at the showdown. But the betting is light so he exerts a little pressure by announcing a raise and betting $4—that's $2 for the call and $2 more for the raise. The action is back on Doc and he folds, realizing that it is unlikely both Annie and Wild Bill are bluffing with weak hands. As

I'll be no showdown loser to this pair.

LEFT
Jesse prepares to see the showdown between two opponents, Wild Bill and Annie.

❖ LET'S LOOK AT THE TABLE ❖

it happens, his A kicker is higher than Wild Bill's 10 so his hand is marginally the stronger, but he also has to consider Annie.

Annie now faces a bet of $2 to call Wild Bill's raise, otherwise he wins the pot. She doesn't feel that Wild Bill has made a very strong hand, but her two pair is not so powerful to warrant a re-raise because she may have misread the situation. So she calls the $2 bet and triggers a showdown with Wild Bill, hoping she will win but not confident of victory. As it is, her two pair, 10s and 9s, is superior to Wild Bill's one pair of Ks and she scoops the pot of $16.50.

This example illustrates some of the strategic thinking that occurs during a game as players try to assimilate information to make good betting decisions. In Draw, the number of cards each player exchanges can provide clues to the possible strength of your opponents' hands. The betting patterns also help but, with only two betting rounds to negotiate, opportunities are limited compared to other poker games.

One additional point to bear in mind is that the opening bet in Draw poker is often restricted to "Jacks or better," meaning that a player must indicate that his hand contains the equivalent of at least a pair of jacks after the deal or fold. That player would normally act first in the second round of betting too, after the draw. Though these rules are traditional, they are becoming less fashionable.

FIVE-CARD STUD

After Draw poker, Five-Card Stud is the other classic variation of the game with which non-poker players are most likely to be familiar. It remains a fixture in clubs, homes, and online, although it is arguably less exciting than Seven-Card Stud or Texas Hold 'Em versions of the game.

The game begins with each player receiving just two cards, the first face down (which only they can look at), and the second face up, after which there is a betting round. Those players continuing in the game receive their third card face up, before engaging in a further betting round. The pattern is repeated when the fourth and fifth cards are dealt, also face up. Ultimately, any players participating in a showdown at the end of the game will have one card face down, the "hole card," and four cards showing face up. This means that there is plenty of information available as the game develops but, with four betting rounds to negotiate, it can be expensive to see it through to the end. To illustrate how it works, let's rejoin our friends at the poker table.

What a calamity! I've got to fold again, darn it.

Doc is the dealer on this occasion and the game is a $1–$2 fixed-limit affair, the opening two rounds requiring bets in increments of a dollar, and the last two rounds subject to a $2 minimum stake. All players have put in their antes of 50 cents each. Working clockwise around the table as usual, Doc deals each player their down, or hole, card, then deals them another, face up. The first player to bet is the one holding the highest value card on display and, in the opening round of betting only, checking is not an option. If two or more players are showing equally high value cards, then the first of these to the dealer's left opens the betting.

Doc himself has an A hearts showing and so he opens the betting for $1. Betting continues clockwise around the table so the action is on Annie who has the Q clubs showing and the 8 hearts as her hole card. Annie needs a 9, 10, J to make a straight, which is possible but unlikely. Also, although a pair is often enough to win a hand in stud, she knows that pairing her Q may not be sufficient to claim the pot, and with another Q on the table in front of Jesse, her hand is looking weak. Annie folds.

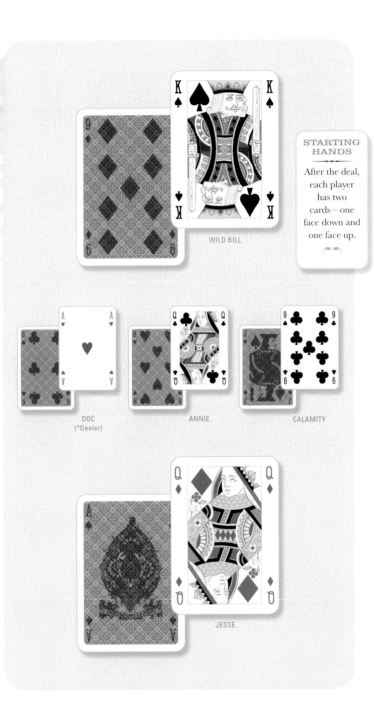

WILD BILL

DOC
(*Dealer)

ANNIE

CALAMITY

JESSE

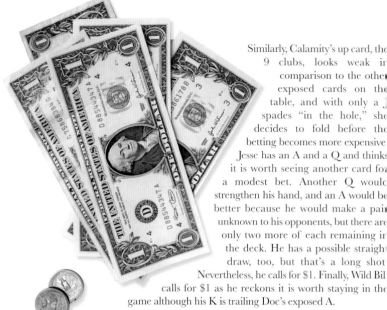

Similarly, Calamity's up card, the 9 clubs, looks weak in comparison to the other exposed cards on the table, and with only a J spades "in the hole," she decides to fold before the betting becomes more expensive. Jesse has an A and a Q and thinks it is worth seeing another card for a modest bet. Another Q would strengthen his hand, and an A would be better because he would make a pair unknown to his opponents, but there are only two more of each remaining in the deck. He has a possible straight draw, too, but that's a long shot. Nevertheless, he calls for $1. Finally, Wild Bill calls for $1 as he reckons it is worth staying in the game although his K is trailing Doc's exposed A.

THIRD STREET

So, two players have folded and there is $5.50 in the pot as Doc deals a third card, face up, to Jesse, Wild Bill, and himself. Now Wild Bill has a pair of Ks showing and he starts the betting for this round since he has the best visible hand. It looks strong but Doc has also been dealt a K, meaning there is only one remaining in the deck. Had Wild Bill raised during the first betting round, he may have suggested to the others that he had that other K as his hole card, which might have given him the chance to impose more pressure. But he didn't, so he decides to bet $1 on the basis that he has the best hand showing and it is up to the others to force him out of the game.

Doc thinks it unlikely that Wild Bill has the other K and his A could therefore prove valuable. He decides to raise, implying that his hole card is an A and that he has been keeping quiet about it. He puts $2 in the pot—$1 for the call and $1 for the raise itself. The J clubs provides Jesse with the chance of drawing a straight, but he is more concerned that he has yet to make a pair and will need at least a pair of As to beat what is on the table. As Doc has the A hearts showing and is betting to suggest he may have another in the hole, Jesse suspects he will struggle, particularly as the bet of $2 to call is relatively large and the next two betting rounds are for higher stakes. Jesse folds.

THE GOLDEN RULE
◆

Wild Bill is breaking the golden rule of Five-Card Stud, namely, that if you are already losing to a hand you can see on the table, you should fold. Following this advice could save you money and help to avoid facing some awkward decisions.

DOC

JESSE

THIRD STREET

The remaining players' hands after the third card has been dealt.

❧

WILD BILL

WILD BILL

DOC

FOUR
STRE

Fourth
brings
players
Neither
is impr
though
could tr
flush c

WILD BILL

FIFTH
STREET

Fifth street
brings Doc
another 7.
He can only
win the pot
by bluffing.

DOC

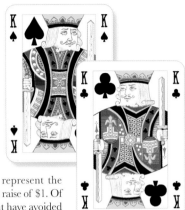

Now Wild Bill has a problem. Does Doc have an A in the hole? He didn't represent it in the first betting round but could have been playing it slowly since, as the first to act in that round, a sizeable bet then may have persuaded his opponents to fold and reduced any potential winnings. Equally, as Doc can see Wild Bill's pair of Ks and knows there is only one K left in the deck, Wild Bill figures that Doc will play on his doubts by continuing to represent the additional A. Wild Bill decides to call the raise of $1. Of course, if he had folded earlier, he might have avoided this tricky situation.

FOURTH STREET

Both players receive their next card face up and they each have a 7. Doc has the 7 hearts to add to the A and K hearts already showing, but Wild Bill's 7 diamonds doesn't help him. The pressure is still on as Wild Bill bets the minimum $2, now the limit has been raised for the third betting round. Doc could raise to suggest he is now drawing a flush but, having already represented the A with a raise, he thinks Wild Bill will see through this. He calls, hoping for an A with the fifth card.

THE SHOWDOWN

The last card is dealt with the 10 hearts doing nothing for Wild Bill and the 7 clubs giving Doc a pair of 7s. Wild Bill is still first to bet with the best visible hand but, if he checks, Doc may bet to continue representing his hole card as an A, which would give him two pair. And if Wild Bill bets, he faces the same dilemma if Doc re-raises. Doc knows that he is losing to the pair of Ks and will only win with a bluff, reinforcing the idea that his hole card is an A and giving Wild Bill a chance to fold.

After a moment's deliberation, Wild Bill bets $2, Doc re-raises him $2, and Wild Bill reluctantly calls because, having already put $7.50 in the pot, he is determined not to give it up. The players reveal their hands, with Wild Bill's pair of Ks beating Doc's pair of 7s.

This example shows how more betting rounds can swell the pot very quickly and it also reveals some of the decisions you may face. Wild Bill did not know he was ahead when he paired the K and could have folded at any time under pressure from Doc. Equally, Doc could have folded when he fell behind in the game but, in persisting with his bluff, he demonstrated that he was prepared to gamble. His opponents will be uncertain whether he is bluffing or not the next time he comes out betting.

TEXAS HOLD 'EM EXAMPLE

Having taken a basic look at two classic poker variants, it's time to consider the game responsible for expanding interest in poker around the world—Texas Hold 'Em, or Hold 'Em for short. It has been suggested that the world of poker is currently in love with Hold 'Em and it is the variant played to determine the world champion at the World Series of Poker. We will deal with Texas Hold 'Em in more detail in the next chapter, but will look here at the basic structure of the game.

To start the game, each player is dealt two cards, face down, as their hole cards. After a round of betting comes the "flop," which is the term for the three cards the dealer reveals, face up, in the center of the table. All players can count these community cards with the two in their hand to make a five-card poker hand. After another round of betting, the dealer reveals a fourth card, face up, known as "fourth street," meaning that players can now see six cards from which to make their five-card hand. A further betting round is followed by the revealing of the final community card, "the river," which the dealer again places face up on the table. After a final betting round, the player who makes the best five-card poker hand from any combination of his two hole cards and the five community cards is the winner. It is perfectly OK for players to dismiss their hole cards from the equation and just use the community cards. This is called "playing the board."

BEFORE THE FLOP

In order to explain the mechanics of Hold 'Em and a few of the game's key components, let's drop in on our buddies at the table once more as they play a $2–$4 fixed-limit game. In this case, the first two betting rounds require bets in $2 denominations, with the last two rounds requiring minimum bets of $4. Annie, in seat three, is dealing. The two players to her immediate left must make a compulsory bet each, known as a "blind," before they see any cards. Calamity, first to Annie's left, posts the "small blind," typically $1 in a $2–$4 limit game, and Jesse posts the "big blind" of $2. This method of ensuring there is a pot to contest differs from Draw and Five-Card Stud, where each player is expected to ante-up at the beginning of the hand.

Annie deals two cards face down to each of the players, who then look at these cards before the betting begins for real. Of course, they do not know what cards their opponents possess as they attempt to make the best poker hand they can from the seven cards potentially available to them by the end of the game.

As Calamity and Jesse have already made their compulsory blind bets, Wild Bill is now required to make a betting decision. He can call the $2 blind, raise, or fold but he cannot check because the first two players have already made a bet. Wild Bill has a K hearts and a J diamonds, referred to as K J "offsuit" because the suits do not match. It's a fair hand but not powerful, so Wild Bill calls for $2.

CALAMITY

JESSE

WILD BILL

DOC

BEFORE THE FLOP

Each players' hand is shown after the deal, but before the flop.

ANNIE
(*Dealer)

✺ LET'S LOOK AT THE TABLE ✺

Doc is looking at a pair of Qs, a very strong "starting hand," inferior only to a pair of As or a pair of Ks at this stage. He doesn't believe that anybody has either of these so he raises with a total bet of $4–$2 to call and $2 for the raise. This is enough to persuade Annie to fold her J 2 offsuit, which is a poor hand. She thinks Doc must have a pair or perhaps two cards higher than a J; either way she is behind so folds. Note, as she was not obliged to make a bet, she has not lost any money at all in this hand.

Calamity, who bet the small blind of $1, must bet $3 to call Doc. She has J 10 offsuit, a moderate hand with some potential, and decides to call. The 7 6 offsuit held by Jesse is also a moderate hand but, like Calamity, he sees that the two consecutive cards he holds could help make up a straight and, since he has already had to bet $2 as the big blind, he adds a further $2 to call Doc as well. Now Wild Bill must decide whether to call for the additional $2 and, although he thinks Doc may have a pair, he calls the bet.

Before the flop, the dealer "burns" the top card by placing it at the bottom of the deck to help counteract cheating through the recognition of marked cards. For instance, if Doc knew that the top card to be revealed was a Q he would gain an unfair advantage over his opponents. Annie deals the flop and the cards revealed are 5 diamonds, 8 spades, and K clubs.

CALAMITY

JESSE

WILD BILL

DOC

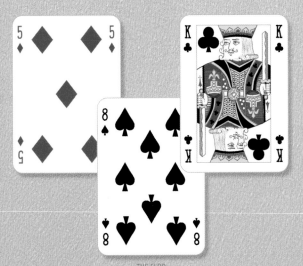

THE FLOP

THE FLOP

The second betting round begins with Calamity to the dealer's immediate left, who may check, bet or fold. The flop hasn't improved her hand and she will probably fold, but at this point she may as well check as she can always fold later in the round if somebody makes a bet she doesn't wish to match. If everybody checks then she is still in the game and "fourth street" will be revealed for free.

Jesse likes the flop as it offers the opportunity for a straight. The 5 8 on the board with the 7 6 in his hand gives him an "up-and-down straight draw," meaning that any 9 or 4 will complete the straight and possibly make him a winner. But he feels cautious and checks. Wild Bill suspects that Doc has a pair but he likes his pair of Ks so he bets $2, at which point Doc makes a bold move by raising another $2. Calamity now takes her chance to fold but Jesse calls Doc's bet of $4, thinking there may be some benefit in pursuing his straight draw. Finally, Wild Bill calls the extra $2.

> Ladies and gentlemen, it's time for a bold move.

FOURTH STREET

RIVER CARD

FOURTH STREET

Annie deals the fourth community card—"fourth street"—and this is a 9 clubs. For Jesse, now first to bet, the 9 completes his straight—5 6 7 8 9— and he makes the minimum bet of $4 now that the limit has been raised. Wild Bill can see that a straight is possible and has noted Jesse's betting patterns. He knows that if Jesse has made his straight, then even a K as the fifth community card will not help him and so he decides to fold.

Doc can also see that Jesse may have a straight, but he is emotionally attached to his pair of Qs and the money already bet, so he calls Jesse's $4 bet.

THE RIVER

Annie deals the fifth community card—the "river"—which is the A spades, and Jesse can see that his hand is unbeatable. Unless Doc also has a 7 6 in his hand to match Jesse, the best he can hold is three As—two in his hand and one from the board, giving him only three of a kind. Jesse has "the nuts," meaning that he possesses the best hand possible from the cards available. To finish the betting, Jesse checks in the hope that Doc will bet again to swell the pot even more, allowing Jesse to then call for a showdown he must win. But Doc is wise to this and checks as well, at which point they reveal their hands and Jesse wins the pot.

This example covers the sequence of play in Hold 'Em and is also a good illustration of the changing fortunes of each player. Before the flop, Doc was leading with a pair of Qs, but the flop helped Wild Bill into the lead by providing him with a pair of Ks. Jesse had a "drawing hand," meaning that he had the potential to improve, but was trailing both the others until fourth street. At that point, Jesse took the lead but he couldn't be certain that he would win. In the end, the river card had no impact on the game and Jesse held on. Having understood this, you are ready to look at Texas Hold 'Em in more detail.

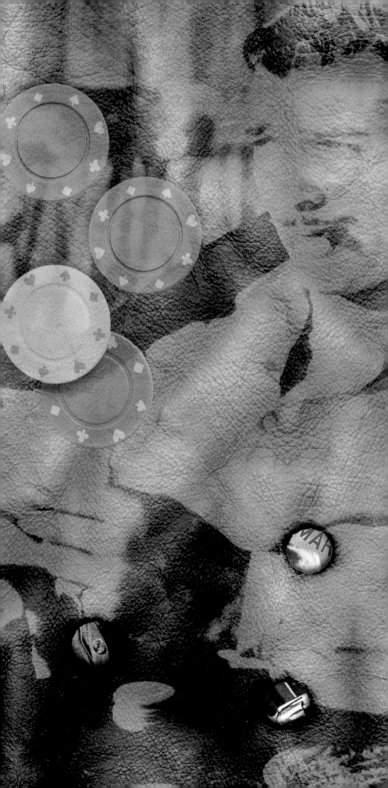

TEXAS HOLD 'EM

In the previous chapter, we concentrated on the basics of poker to help you understand the objectives of the game, how to play, and how the betting is structured as the game progresses. Having looked at the example hands to illustrate three of the most popular variations, you should now be able to appreciate the dynamics of each game and how key strategic or tactical decisions can influence the outcome of a hand. The Five-Card Stud example also demonstrated how holding the strongest hand can still leave a player feeling vulnerable, while holding a weaker hand does not prevent a player from acting aggressively to create doubt in the minds of opponents.

The Texas Hold 'Em illustration revealed the fluctuating fortunes of the competing players as the community cards were exposed. The lead changed hands three times as the game unfolded and it is this degree of volatility that helps Hold 'Em retain its position as the poker game of choice for so many players. This chapter will take a more detailed look at Texas Hold 'Em, highlighting some ideas that may help you improve your game.

LEFT
These cards show a full house. Queens over Aces represent a powerful hand.

BASIC STRATEGY

Texas Hold 'Em is a deceptively simple game that incorporates a wide range of factors that will influence your play as a hand develops. Issues to consider include your position at the table relative to the dealer, the quality of your starting hand, the size of your chip stack, and the levels of skill—and sometimes luck—enjoyed by your opponents. Comprehend how these factors will fluctuate throughout a session and you will notice that one lapse in concentration, or one misreading of a situation, can undo plenty of good play. Absorb the lessons well, however, and you will be able to face the vagaries of poker fortune with a great deal more confidence by exercising control in pressure situations. Starting with the example Hold 'Em hand in the previous chapter, we can analyze some of the strategic considerations our buddies had in mind as they played, pointing out the good, the bad, and the ugly situations that they faced along the way.

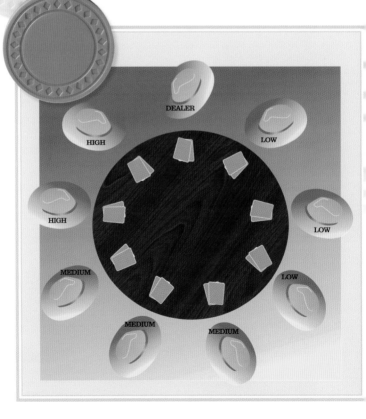

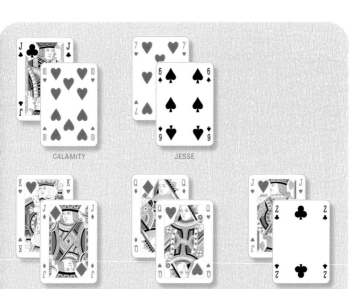

CALAMITY   JESSE

WILD BILL   DOC   ANNIE

TABLE POSITION

Let's first rewind to the point at which the five players receive their starting hands, or hole cards, and explain what they have in mind as they contemplate their betting decisions. The game, remember, was a $2–$4 fixed-limit affair.

As Calamity and Jesse were "in the blinds," Wild Bill has the first betting decision to make as he looks at his K J offsuit. He is in "mid-position," as third player from the dealer, and this is tricky for him. In a casino game that could have as many as nine players at a table, players in "early position" would be the three to the dealer's immediate left, the first two of whom will have posted the blinds. The next three or four players would consider themselves in "mid-position" and the remainder, including the dealer of course, would be in "late position," always an advantage because of the opportunity to glean information from those acting ahead of you in the betting rounds.

Wild Bill's first problem is that he has no information from Calamity and Jesse, to his left, because they had to bet without first seeing their hands, and he obviously has no clues yet regarding the strength of hands held by the players behind him. His picture cards may look pretty, but anyone holding an A is already beating him, and the more players there are at the table, the more likely it is that someone will have at least a bare A. But it's a decent hand that may be worth a call, keeping him alive in the game. Should another player represent a stronger hand with a raise, he could fold for a loss of only $2.

OPENING CONSIDERATIONS

Doc's pair of Qs is very strong. It's a premium starting hand, and definitely worth supporting. But how should he play it? As it is bettered only by a pair of As or Ks, he could support it strongly to make his opponents with weak or average hands fold, thus improving his chances by reducing the competition. If he makes a large enough bet, everybody else might fold although, because of his position at the table, he will pick up a modest pot. This may seem a waste of a good opportunity yet, if he merely calls to disguise the quality of his hand in the hope of capitalizing on it later, he is vulnerable to anybody holding an A or a K. The appearance of an A or K on the flop would present him with much more to consider. As it is, Doc makes a small raise by betting $4.

Annie, of course, quite rightly folded her J 2 offsuit which is a worthless starting hand. Though it is true that poorer hands can be supported when in late position, it is best to do this if the chance to see the flop comes cheap. Should there be several calls before the flop but no raises, there will be more value in calling. Under the circumstances, with two players having already supported their hands after seeing their cards, she makes a good decision. Assuming Doc has a pair, she reasons that even a J on the flop could still leave her well behind without many chances of winning.

I've had to make some tough decisions, but this sure as darn it tops them all.

For Calamity, her first decision is whether to give up her $1 blind. Having made a compulsory bet, it is easy to fall into the trap of believing that you simply have to play, whatever cards you hold, in order to have a run for your money. Play for higher stakes, as you will if you reach tournament level, and saying adios to a blind of a hundred bucks without seeing the flop is something you'll have to contemplate. However much it hurts, sometimes it's the best policy. Calamity, of course, only has to call $3 in this game and with a J 10 offsuit, she has an up-and-down straight draw. If an A, K, and Q appear on the board, she'll have the best straight and, more importantly, may see plenty of betting action from opponents holding any of these cards, or even a pair of them, in their hand. Three of a kind is inferior to a straight, don't forget.

CALAMITY

JESSE

WILD BILL

DOC

ANNIE

STARTING HANDS

To recap, here are the
players' starting hands
once again.

JESSE'S AND WILD BILL'S POSITIONS

Jesse's decision to support his big blind is perhaps easier to consider because he only has to call for an additional $2, which doesn't seem much when he's already put that sum in the pot. Again, loosen your attachment to the blinds and you'll probably make better poker decisions. But if you sense value in contesting a multihanded pot with plenty of calls but no raises, go ahead. The 7 6 offsuit gives Jesse an opportunity to exploit a bit of value because, in assuming that Wild Bill, Doc, and Calamity are holding high cards, the low- to middle-ranking cards that can help him may be of no use to his opponents and catapult him into the lead. They will have little idea what sort of hand he has at this stage even if they read the motivation behind his bet correctly.

When Wild Bill calls Doc's $2 raise to conclude the betting before the flop, he is essentially thinking along the same lines as Jesse. Of course, he is vulnerable to any A that may appear on the flop, but he reasons that he should support his initial bet in the interests of value. Even so, Doc's raise could mean that he has an Ace with a K kicker, which would be difficult for him to overtake, or even a pair of Aces.

ABOVE
Wild Bill holds two picture cards: K J offsuit.

RIGHT
Jesse holds 7 6 offsuit.

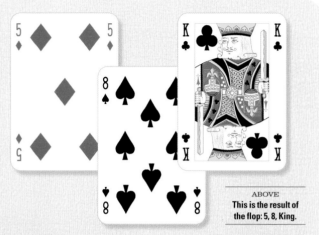

ABOVE
This is the result of
the flop: 5, 8, King.

THE FLOP

The flop, of course, is 5 diamonds, 8 spades, K clubs. Now we can see the problem Calamity faced in supporting her small blind. She checks, expecting to fold should anybody else bet, and accepts that her hand was not that strong from the outset. Unfortunately, she realizes she is going to sacrifice an additional $3 when she could have limited her losses to a buck, and minimizing losses is crucial to playing profitable poker.

The flop proves very helpful to Jesse as the low cards he was hoping to see have materialized, giving him a decent chance of making his straight while they are likely to be of no use to Wild Bill and Doc, who led the betting in the previous round. But his hand still only has strong potential, so should he bet? If he ups the stakes considerably with a big bet, he may convince the others that his protection of the blind has paid off and a low pair of 5s or 8s has been upgraded to three of a kind, often called "trips" (short for triplets). Should his opponents fold, he will have saved himself the agony of waiting for a 4 or 9 to appear and won a tidy pot with, at this stage, a weak hand of only a K high.

In the event, Jesse checks and waits for the others to make a move. This could be interpreted as weakness on Jesse's part, but he knows his opponents will be wary of his advantageous position in the big blind and may respect him on account of this. Meanwhile, Wild Bill's decision to call Doc's raise before the flop seems to have paid off as he now has a pair of Ks. Wild Bill feels he is probably ahead unless Doc has As or, even less likely, Ks in his hand; OK, he may have a pair of 8s or 5s in the hole but Wild Bill believes that Doc would not have raised in mid-position with such a low holding, so he feels more confident. If he bets big, anyone holding less than a pair of Ks is going to fold and he will ask a serious question of anyone holding an A, particularly if backed by a low kicker. But A 8 or A 5 could still cause problems so he makes a "feeler" bet and waits.

PREMIUM STARTING HANDS

In Texas Hold 'Em, your starting hand consists of just two cards, not many on which to make a betting decision. However, the odds of probability being what they are, the list of hands below can be supported whatever position you hold at the table—early, mid, or late. They are not unbeatable since the flop can undermine any starting hand, but they do present you with a potential advantage.

Play any starting hands apart from these and you may win, but it can be hard work.

BIG PAIRS
As, Ks, Qs

MEDIUM PAIRS
Js, 10s, 9s

SMALL PAIRS
8s or lower

SUITED CARDS
AK, AQ, AJ, A10, KQ, KJ, K10, QJ, Q10, J10, J9, 10 9

UNSUITED CARDS
AK, AQ, AJ, A10, KQ, KJ

BETTING AFTER THE FLOP

Doc sees that his pair of Qs is weakened by the presence of the K on the board and the chance that one of his opponents has a K in their hand. Now the value of betting heavily before the flop becomes apparent as he visualizes his strong starting hand disappearing down the drain along with his chips. He realizes, correctly, that he will probably need a Q to put him back in front and the odds of that happening are poor, with only two of the other 47 cards to help him. He should probably fold now and wait for the next opportunity, but he makes another raise.

Calamity takes her cue and rightly folds but Jesse is not discouraged by the size of the bet because he knows that he has eight cards working for him. If another K, 8, or 5 appears to "pair the board," he might worry about someone getting a full house. But the chances of a flush coming up are low given the assortment of suits on the flop. Jesse calls Doc's bet although a checkraise isn't out of the question. This would constitute a semi-bluff, a phrase coined by poker theorist David Sklansky, whereby Jesse knows he is behind but, if he bets and is called, he still has chances to win.

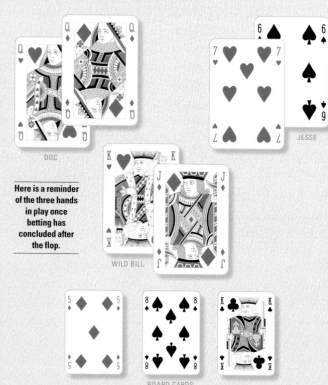

DOC

JESSE

Here is a reminder of the three hands in play once betting has concluded after the flop.

WILD BILL

BOARD CARDS

FLOPS, FULL HOUSES, AND FLUSHES

In Hold 'Em remember that, with only two hole cards, it is not possible to make a full house unless a pair appears on the board. For example, if you start with a pair of As, you need another A plus a pair of another value on the board for a full house. However, if the board displays three 9s and an A, you will have a strong full house but will still lose to someone holding the other 9. It's unlikely, but it can happen. Similarly, a flush can only be possible if the board shows at least three cards of the same suit.

ABOVE
A pair of Aces—the strongest starting hand in Hold 'Em.

ABOVE
The Aces above matched with these board cards constitutes a full house—Aces over 9s.

RIGHT
However, somebody may be holding a pair of 9s, giving them four of a kind— which beats a full house!

75

FOURTH STREET

Wild Bill calls the bet as well, with his pair of Ks, and the "turn" card, or fourth street, is revealed.

This was the 9 clubs, just the card Jesse wanted to see and one that puts him in the lead for this hand. Even someone holding three of a kind would be behind him so he is in a very strong position to make a bet and close the hand out now, probably the most advisable course of action. If he waits in the hope of milking more money from his opponents, he takes the risk of running into a flush, or even a straight flush, if another club falls on the river. Plus, if the river card pairs the board instead, he could be staring down the barrel of an unlikely full house. But Jesse bets the minimum $4.

Wild Bill has been monitoring Jesse's betting patterns and figures that he probably has made the straight. He knows that Jesse could have been calling for value with any two cards before the flop when matching Doc's raise. After the flop, Jesse checked as though not having a strong hand, but happily called Doc's bet once more, suggesting that he must have something worthwhile to keep him interested, perhaps two pair of 8s and 5s for instance. Now the 9 clubs is showing, two pair, perhaps Ks and 9s, is possible, but the straight is out there for anyone holding 7 6, and that would prove too good for Wild Bill, who can only manage three Ks at best. Seeing that he could be beaten already, Wild Bill takes the sensible option and folds, forfeiting the $8 he put into the pot without feeling compelled to throw good money after bad.

DOC

JESSE

WILD BILL

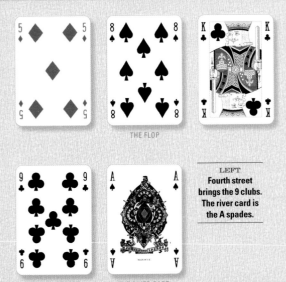

THE FLOP

LEFT
Fourth street brings the 9 clubs. The river card is the A spades.

FOURTH STREET   THE RIVER CARD

If Doc has a pair of As in his hand after all, then he isn't even running second at the moment. It's a good decision. As his pair of Qs looks more unappealing, Doc realizes that Jesse could simply be holding a K and that would be enough to win as things stand. If he had folded after the flop, recognizing that it not only didn't fit his hand, but actually threatened it, he wouldn't be in this mess. Now he is the only player who can stop Jesse winning the pot but he probably doesn't have the cards to do so. Again, he can see the straight possibility and knows that another Q won't help, but he recklessly calls anyway.

THE RIVER

When the river card, the A spades, is dealt, Jesse knows he has the best possible hand, "the nuts," and will win the pot. But does he bet enough to tempt Doc into calling with a losing hand? Or should he bet big and encourage Doc to fold? He could check in the hope that Doc bets again, at which point he could re-raise and see Doc fold then, a few chips lighter. The benefit of betting to avoid showing his hand is not lost on Jesse, but he decides to check. When Doc checks, having pursued a lost cause for far too long, the showdown reveals that Jesse is the winner, having started with a couple of pretty low-ranking cards. The fact that they were "connected" provided Jesse with the impetus he needed to play and, after the flop, he had even more reason to hang in there.

PLAYING THE FLOP

The detailed look at our friends' game helps to illustrate some of the thought processes that must be taken into consideration while playing Texas Hold 'Em. By analyzing each hand in turn, it is possible to appreciate the decisions facing each of the players as the betting unfolds. The point is, when playing for real, you won't know what cards your opponents are holding. That, of course, is what makes poker so exhilarating every time you have to make a decision. So let's look more closely at possible starting hands, both good and indifferent, to help you appreciate how their value can fluctuate after the flop. As Don discovered with his pair of Qs, even a lovely pair of ladies can soon become a liability if not played right.

Picture yourself holding a pair of As before the flop. You feel impregnable since with only two cards dealt to each player you must have the top starting hand. But how strong is the hand really? Let's look at some example flops—good, bad and ugly—to find out.

SLOW PLAYING A HAND

The term "slow playing" does not refer to a player who takes an incredibly long time to make a decision at the poker table. Rather, it describes the playing of a strong hand in such a fashion as to disguise its true merit. Imagine you have a pair of 7s and are first to bet when the flop is A K 7. By checking, you are hoping that anyone with an A or K will read your hand as weak and bet, leaving you free to trap them with a raise. If nobody bets, then you are probably way ahead and can bide your time, playing your hand slowly in an effort to maximize the winnings.

YOUR HAND

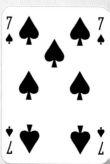

FLOP CARDS

YOUR HAND

FLOP CARDS

◆ THE GOOD... ◆

This is a good flop and presents you with a great winning opportunity since you can expect anyone holding a K to come out betting, particularly if they have a big kicker. Hands such as AK, KQ, or KJ are what you want to be playing against. Bet strongly here and you will be asking some tough questions of your opponents. You might run into someone holding a pair of 8s or 6s if really unlucky but, if you'd made a big enough bet before the flop, they may well have folded already.

YOUR HAND

FLOP CARDS

◆ THE BAD... ◆

Now this is a bad flop for a pair of As since anyone with a KQ, KJ, or K10 is obviously way ahead. Hell, someone may even be holding one of the other As with a K, or perhaps they gambled with a poor K 7 as their hole cards and got lucky. If you bet and are raised, you've probably lost your chips; if you check and there's a bet, at least you can throw the As away relatively cheaply. But if you're in late position and the action has been checked to you, what do you do then? A big bet could be met with a checkraise from someone "slow playing" a K, and that can hurt. It's best to check and hope they've missed the flop too or, that you get lucky with another A on the turn or river.

YOUR HAND

FLOP CARDS

◆ THE UGLY... ◆

An ugly situation for your hand since someone could have made a flush (with two more diamonds) or a straight (with any K 10 or, less likely, 10 8) already, or they could at least be looking at a flush or straight draw. You have anyone holding a Q or J covered, but Q J is a reasonable starting hand and you could be up against two pair. In this instance, a 9 may help you and an A would be better. But how will you feel if the A diamonds comes up on fourth street? Your three of a kind is now definitely under threat from a flush and if someone bets as though they've hit it, are you ready to gamble on pairing the board for your full house?

YOUR HAND

FLOP CARDS

◆ THE NOT SO UGLY.... ◆

Once again you have an "overpair" to the flop. Something like A 10 or A 7 is a possible holding for an opponent who bets into you, meaning that the action is on him and he is pressurizing you with a bet. The obvious response is a raise. You certainly don't want to let an opponent see the turn card (fourth street) cheaply and watch an A appear. That's going to hurt, as would seeing, say, another 10 on the board, offering the chance for you to "trip up" on trip 10s, three of a kind. The Ks present an opportunity and a flop like this should encourage you to take it.

YOUR HAND   FLOP CARDS

◆ AND THE PRETTY UGLY... ◆

Not the ugliest flop, but pretty bad, nonetheless. Anyone holding an
A is ahead and A Q against you is quite possible. Your betting
position is important here since, if you are first to act, you have the
chance to exert some pressure. Bet enough and even an A with a
low kicker might fold, figuring you for a pair of Qs or an A with a
bigger kicker in the hole. But if you are called, you can be sure you are
behind, so how much are you willing to risk? Another tough decision, but
that's poker. Hang around long enough to see a K clubs on the turn and
suddenly you've got a possible flush or a straight to contend with, despite the
fact that your hand has improved to three of a kind.

OVERPAIRS AND OVERCARDS

An overpair is simply a pair you hold in your hand
that consists of two cards of higher value than any
individual cards on the flop. If you hold a pair of
10s, then you have an overpair to a flop that comes
9 7 4. Similarly, possessing an overcard means that
you have a card in your hand that is of a higher
value than any community cards on the board.

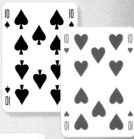

OVERPAIR

FLOP CARDS

YOUR HAND   FLOP CARDS

◆ IT GETS UGLIER... ◆

This flop to your pair of Ks is bad news, with the A on board ugly enough on its own. Since many players will happily bet A with any kicker before the flop, the 9s suddenly take on a new perspective, too, with a full house the worst case scenario opposing you. However, 10 9 or 9 8 suited are perfectly playable hands, particularly if you've let an opponent in cheaply on the flop, and then you're behind trip 9s. If you're playing a nickels and dimes game and someone bets, you'll probably call for the hell of it since not much is at stake. But imagine yourself down to your last $200 in a "No Limit" game and someone bets enough to force you "all-in" if you call? Are you confident enough in your Ks to run the risk of making this your last hand for the evening? Be patient: it's perfectly possible you can win the next pot with a weaker hand than a pair of Ks. Remember, if the flop doesn't fit, fold your hand and wait for another chance.

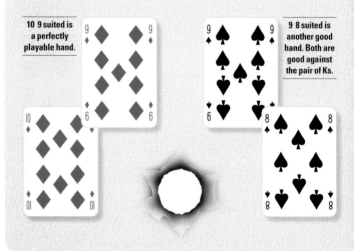

10 9 suited is a perfectly playable hand.

9 8 suited is another good hand. Both are good against the pair of Ks.

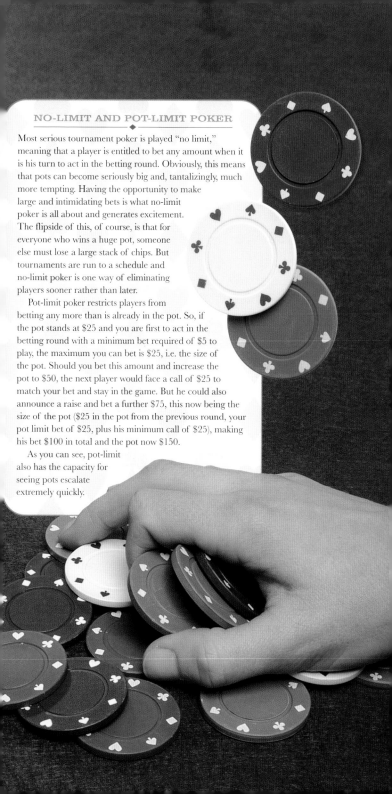

NO-LIMIT AND POT-LIMIT POKER

Most serious tournament poker is played "no limit," meaning that a player is entitled to bet any amount when it is his turn to act in the betting round. Obviously, this means that pots can become seriously big and, tantalizingly, much more tempting. Having the opportunity to make large and intimidating bets is what no-limit poker is all about and generates excitement. The flipside of this, of course, is that for everyone who wins a huge pot, someone else must lose a large stack of chips. But tournaments are run to a schedule and no-limit poker is one way of eliminating players sooner rather than later.

Pot-limit poker restricts players from betting any more than is already in the pot. So, if the pot stands at $25 and you are first to act in the betting round with a minimum bet required of $5 to play, the maximum you can bet is $25, i.e. the size of the pot. Should you bet this amount and increase the pot to $50, the next player would face a call of $25 to match your bet and stay in the game. But he could also announce a raise and bet a further $75, this now being the size of the pot ($25 in the pot from the previous round, your pot limit bet of $25, plus his minimum call of $25), making his bet $100 in total and the pot now $150.

As you can see, pot-limit also has the capacity for seeing pots escalate extremely quickly.

YOUR HAND   FLOP CARDS

◆ "TRAP-CHECKING" AN OPPONENT ◆

Only someone holding a pair of As in their hand could be beating you at the moment so this has to be a good flop. If you're in early position, you could be able to "trap-check" an opponent, provided you think they'll bet on the strength of the A. If not, put in a bet to dissuade any but the foolhardy from calling you. If you're in late position and someone bets, re-raise unless you are convinced they really do have a pair of As.

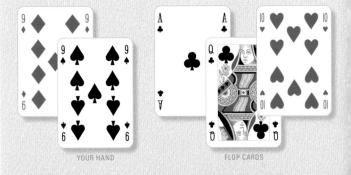

YOUR HAND   FLOP CARDS

◆ THE OUTCOME ◆

A bad flop for your hand this time with three overcards against you and the possibility that someone will be in with a K, J, making a straight. Any A, Q, or 10 is beating you and it's plausible that someone could be holding A, Q for two pair. If a 9 clubs appears on the turn, suddenly the threat of a flush against your trip 9s is all too real and where do you go from there?

ALL-IN

Going "all-in" means simply that you are betting all your chips on the one hand, enabling you to call a bet when you don't possess enough chips to match the full amount. If you hold the best hand, you can only win an amount equal to your total stake from the opponents who continue in that hand. Any additional betting that other players engage in during the hand is referred to as a side pot and concerns only them, even if your hand proves the strongest. If you lose, it's either time to re-buy chips, if permitted, or locate the exit.

In tournament play, those running low on chips are always in danger of having an opponent "put them all-in" by betting sufficient to force them into risking all their remaining chips should they call. It's a bullying tactic, of course, but then the object of tournament play is to amass chips and knock out your opponents.

TRAP-CHECKING

This is the phrase used to describe the tactic of checking to induce a bet from an opponent, before raising when the action returns to you in the betting round. Checking is often a sign of weakness from a player in early position, and the idea is to convey that message to your opponents. You check, they bet, and then you pounce with a big raise. Like most tactical plays in poker, it is most effective when used sparingly and it only works properly if you are confident that at least one of your opponents will like the flop enough to make a bet. Otherwise you could see everyone checking and the turn card appearing for free, and that may seriously improve another player's hand.

The rules state that as I'm all-in, I have to knock out my opponents to win!

YOUR HAND

FLOP CARDS

◆ A GOOD OPPORTUNITY? ◆

On the face of it, this looks like a good opportunity, but it could still turn ugly. Obviously, anyone holding another Q has you cooked, but what about other overpairs to your hand—As, Ks, Js, and 10s? If you bet and someone raises you, what do you do? You need a 9, but if they have got a Q, then you could still find yourself saddled with a losing full house and a cast iron opportunity to reduce your chip stack.

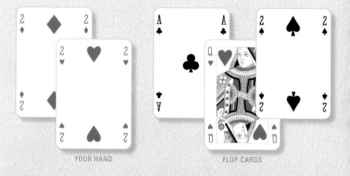

YOUR HAND

FLOP CARDS

◆ THINGS TO CONSIDER ◆

Playing low pairs such as 2s can be worthwhile but it's not really a raising hand before the flop unless you're feeling bold. This is because you are probably going to need plenty of help to win should an opponent call. In this example, a 2 on the flop is going to look insignificant to anyone holding an A and that presents you with your chance. You should be thinking of betting big or, if you are in late position, consider re-raising any bet to close out the hand there and then.

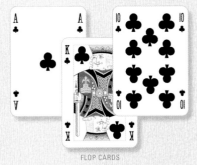

YOUR HAND   FLOP CARDS

◆ AN EXTREMELY BAD FLOP ◆

This is an extreme example of a bad flop to your pair of 2s, but it emphasizes the problems you can face in playing them. Three overcards, a flush draw, and a straight for anyone holding Q J represent a fair number of chances to lose. You cannot feel confident in this position if somebody makes a move on you, although you may be tempted to play aggressively and post an audacious bet if you're in early position. That may be just enough to scare away somebody holding an A or K with a small kicker. It's risky though, especially if you're up against anyone reluctant to throw away an A they've paired on the board. They will call for certain.

AGGRESSIVE PLAY

Strong, aggressive play generally requires players to bet heavily or re-raise on the flop to test the nerves of their opponents. A combination of three high cards on the board is often referred to as a "raiser's flop" because players will assume that somebody has benefited and will raise the level of betting accordingly. Of course, such a flop also presents an opportunity to scare opponents with a bluff and that represents really aggressive play.

RAISER'S FLOP

YOUR HAND   FLOP CARDS

◆ SUPPORTING LOW PAIRS ◆

This is very ugly and, again, shows the problem with supporting low pairs. Aggressive play may get you out of trouble but, realistically, there are too many playable hands out there that could be ahead of you. Ignoring the Ks for a moment, A 9 offsuit, 10 9 suited, maybe even 9 8 suited are all possible starting hands for your opponents. Any bet against you will leave you praying for a 2 and that's not good for your health.

YOUR HAND   FLOP CARDS

◆ THE "BIG SLICK" ◆

A K, the "big slick," is a very strong starting hand since any A or K on the flop brings you the likely top pair with top kicker. Anyone holding A Q, A J, or A 10 will be keen to bet. There is the danger of A 8 or A 5 being out there but, in this example, with the A K suited, the clubs on the board give you a strong flush draw as insurance. Bet aggressively and you'll probably take the pot.

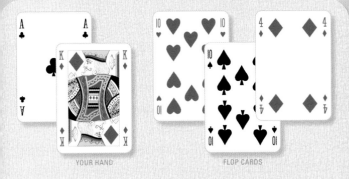

YOUR HAND   FLOP CARDS

◆ LOSING POWER ◆

A bad flop with the A K offsuit not looking as powerful now as it did when you first looked at your cards. Three 10s is the obvious worry since A 10, K 10, or even J 10 are possible hands against you. A 4 is not unlikely either, leaving you in an awkward spot. You won't want to bet too hastily here, and raising an opponent's bet will take plenty of courage. Of course, A K is a hand that could encourage you to raise before the flop, but this example illustrates how such optimism can turn sour. You just have to accept that such a gamble doesn't always pay off.

YOUR HAND   FLOP CARDS

◆ SERIOUSLY UGLY ◆

Here things are even uglier than in the previous example. If someone bets on this flop you'd have to assume they have at least paired the board. A 8, A 7, or A 6 are clearly dangerous and connecting cards such as 10 9 or even 5 4 are attractive propositions for those players hoping to see a cheap flop. The truth is, though, that you don't really know where you are in this hand. Having overcards may look encouraging but, unless you fancy a bit of "loose play," it is advisable to fold quietly.

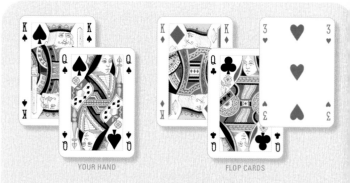

YOUR HAND   FLOP CARDS

◆ WATCH 'EM FOLD ◆

Two pair on the flop is always a good sight and you have any A K or A Q in trouble in this situation, let alone anyone playing an A with a low kicker. Serious betting action before the flop can dispose of anyone holding a low pair, rendering the chance of finding yourself against trip 3s unlikely. And anyone playing loose enough to be in with K 3 or Q 3, poor starting hands without doubt, is still well held. Bet strongly and not many players will immediately read you for holding the top two pair. If you're in late position and an opponent bets, a sizeable re-raise should earn you sufficient respect for them to fold.

YOUR HAND   FLOP CARDS

◆ TRICKY DECISIONS ◆

This example of a bad flop to your hand encapsulates many of the points raised before. Any hand with an A is ahead and a player holding A K or A Q will be eagerly looking for some betting action. Yes, a Q could come on fourth street but you don't want it to be the Q hearts as that would bring all manner of straight and flush possibilities, making your betting decisions even trickier.

TIGHT PLAYERS, LOOSE PLAYERS, AND MANIACS

These are all terms to describe players and playing styles. Some players will fall strictly into one category or another whenever they sit down at the poker table, while others will incorporate elements of all three styles during a session. Tight players support only top-quality hands, exercising caution and risking as little as possible. Loose players, in contrast, have a willingness to gamble when the odds are against them. This attitude can pay off handsomely when hitting an unlikely winning hand, such as a flush or low straight draw that nobody saw coming. But playing too loose too often can quickly decimate your chip stack. If that really doesn't bother you, then you have the potential to be a maniac. Maniacs make the game unpredictable and exciting because they are either blind to the possibility of losing or simply revel in confounding accepted poker wisdom. That makes them dangerous.

TIGHT PLAYER'S HAND

FLOP CARDS

LOOSE PLAYER'S HAND

FLOP CARDS

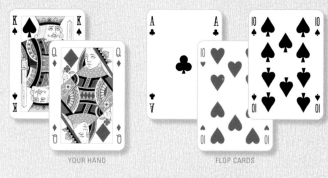

YOUR HAND

FLOP CARDS

◆ POSSIBLY NOT THE BEST TIME ◆

The ugly thing about this flop is that it looks so tempting, with any J giving you the A-high straight. But how much will you have to pay to see it on the turn or river, and what happens if it doesn't materialize? If a K or Q comes on the turn, you will still be behind anyone holding an A. So a J offers the best chance of salvation, but that gives you just four cards from 47 nominally in your favor. True, sometimes you're going to feel like a gamble, especially if you haven't seen a decent starting hand for a while. But this may not be the best time to try a speculative move.

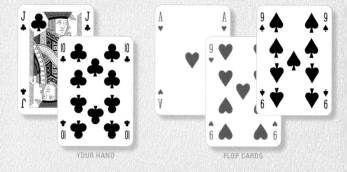

YOUR HAND

FLOP CARDS

◆ THE DANGERS OF MEDIUM-STRENGTH HANDS ◆

To conclude this look at starting hands and playing the flop, let's consider a couple of medium-strength hands and the dangers of playing them. The J 10 offsuit facing a flop like this encourages the optimist to see an up-and-down straight draw since K Q, Q 8 or 8 7 would all help if appearing on the turn and the river. However, if a K comes on the turn, that may have made someone two pair, and someone else may already have an A. So the cost of playing on in the hand could easily become prohibitive the longer you hang around.

YOUR HAND

FLOP CARDS

◆ TRY A LATE POSITION ◆

A hand like 7 6 suited is best played in late position when you have some information from the betting patterns of the other players. It's not a hand you'll often feel like raising with before the flop. The example shows the potential benefits of playing it, with a middle pair and a flush draw to soothe the nerves. But you are going to come up against overcards like the Q on a regular basis when playing a hand like this, and someone at the table may well have the A or K hearts along with a Q or 7. That means your flush, even if you make it, may be outdrawn by a bigger example, and that is a very ugly occurrence.

OVERCARD

With 7 6 suited, this overcard is a potential threat. Also, if a heart appears, player 1 beats you; and if a 7 appears, player 2's full house is a winner.

PLAYER 1

PLAYER 2

PLAYING THE TURN OR FOURTH STREET

Most poker strategists agree that making a decision when the turn card appears should be relatively easy. In exercising good judgment, most players will have discarded their hands well before this stage on the majority of occasions. Those remaining can be expected to have received some help from the flop or, at least, realized that their opponents are as inconvenienced by it as they are themselves.

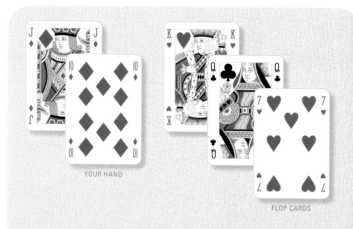

YOUR HAND

FLOP CARDS

◆ PLAYING THE TURN CARD ◆

Problems in playing the turn card usually occur when you have gambled on the flop with cards that ought to have been folded. For example, say you have a J 10 diamonds and the flop is K hearts, Q clubs, and 7 hearts. Yes, a straight draw is a possibility and, if the betting was light after the flop, perhaps you have a chance. But any pair is beating you and if the turn card is, say, a 2 hearts, suddenly you have a flush to worry about and your hand has not improved at all.

TURN CARD

PLAYING THE TURN

The simplest recommendations on playing the turn card are these:

● If the turn card helps strengthen your hand, then bet, raising an opponent if necessary.

● If the turn card leaves you with a drawing hand possibility that can clearly win, then call, provided the betting is not prohibitively expensive.

RIVER CARD

◆ ON THE RIVER ◆

It may be tempting to see the river card, particularly if there are not many contesting the pot and it is cheap to call. But calling repeatedly in situations like this can erode your chip stack. If an A or 9 appears on the river, you've made a straight and could still be losing to someone holding two hearts in their hand. If it's the A or 9 hearts that appears, your straight may still be winning, but how can you bet with confidence knowing that now a flush is an even more likely hand for an opponent?

Should another player bet before you in this instance, you might feel obliged to call for fear that you are being bluffed. After all, you don't want to throw away a possible winning hand having come this far, and therein lies the problem. By staying in the game when you perhaps ought to have folded earlier, you run the risk of seeing your hand improve while still being behind. The pot will appear tantalizingly attractive with perhaps only one opponent left in the hand, and the money you've staked makes it difficult to let go. Bearing that in mind, playing a drawing hand on the turn is only worthwhile if you are confident that you will have the best hand should you hit the right card.

Bluffing on the turn is possible if the board looks favorable, but you'll need to pay attention to the other players and their betting patterns during the hand to assess your chances of pulling it off. If they are poor players, they may not be smart enough to read the bluffing possibilities anyway and you will definitely need the right cards to beat them.

PLAYING THE RIVER

By the time you've seen the river card you will know whether your hand is strong or weak, since all the cards available to you are visible. Opportunities for betting to protect your hand have now gone and your strategy may have to change. Again, if you are confident you have the best hand, then supporting it with a bet is always advisable since it puts pressure on the other players. Two pair will often be good enough to win and three of a kind is peachy. But be wary of those flush and straight draws and, if there is a pair on the board, a full house could be lying in wait for you, too.

Even a top pair with the top kicker is difficult to support in this situation

YOUR HAND

BOARD CARDS

Top pair with top kicker is a difficult hand to bet on at this stage and even the best players will check it, hoping to see a showdown at no extra expense. Yet, if you detect a sign of weakness in a check from an opponent, should you bluff? On the basis that, if you were in their position at this point of the game you'd probably call even with a moderate hand, a naked bluff is unlikely to work. Once again, the key factor in your strategy for playing the river is the pattern of your opponents' betting throughout the hand. Only that will give you any indication of what shape you are in and what betting decision to make. If an opponent checks the action to you, rather than being weak, there is always the possibility that they are encouraging you to swell the pot on their behalf.

That covers the essential factors of Texas Hold 'Em, giving you enough information and ideas on how to play this popular poker variation successfully. More details on the game will follow when considering strategies and tournament play later in the book.

POKER VARIATIONS

Your journey along the poker trail so far has led you through the basic concepts of the game, drawing on the most common variations. You've looked at Draw Poker and Five-Card Stud, the granddaddies of the game, and also the new gunslinger in town, the standard tournament game, Texas Hold 'Em.

Though all are different in style, it is from these games that the majority of other poker variations are derived. For a beginner, these three forms of poker provide plenty of scope for developing an understanding of the game. However, some people have been playing for years and there is always a poker player eager for a new test of skill. With that in mind, let's take a look at several of the more popular and slightly more complex poker variations to have captured the imagination of the world's card players.

RIGHT
"I'm kinda bored takin' your money playin' them easy games. Any of you gentlemen care for Seven-Card Stud?"

SEVEN-CARD STUD

or experienced poker players, Seven-Card Stud vies with Texas Hold 'Em as the most popular variation. The number of cards in the game generates opportunities to build strong hands. Also, with five betting rounds to negotiate before the showdown, the possibility of large pots developing is seductively appealing. But how exactly does Seven-Card Stud work?

Each player, typically having bet a nominal fee for the ante, is dealt three cards, two face down and one face up. There then follows the first round of betting. A fourth card is dealt, face up, to each of those remaining in the hand, followed by another betting round. The pattern continues with the fifth card dealt face up, followed by a betting round, then the sixth card, also dealt face up, and further betting. The seventh card is dealt face down, prior to the final round of betting. Ultimately, two or more players who continue to a showdown will each have seven cards from which to choose their best five-card hand, three of them face down and four face up.

BETTING STRUCTURE
◆

Perhaps the most confusing element of poker is the lack of standardized rules on the betting structure, particularly in the more advanced variations. In Seven-Card Stud, some card schools will insist on antes being compulsory, while others consider the betting so volatile over five rounds that an ante is unnecessary. Equally confusing, opening the betting in the first round is usually the preserve of the player holding the lowest visible card, but some card schools insist this privilege is reserved for the high card, as in Five-Card Stud. As always, the best advice is to be sure of the protocols before you sit down to play.

STARTING HANDS
◆

The strength of your starting hand is crucial in Seven-Card Stud. With your first three cards you want a pair or three of a kind to get ahead of the game. Failing that, suited or consecutive cards that offer flush and straight possibilities can help but, as the hand develops, keep a close eye on the other exposed cards to determine your chances of hitting what you need to win. If you are happy with your starting hand, by fifth street you should be able to reassess your chances. Going beyond this stage demands that you have your hand already or a favorable chance of improving to win.

STARTING HANDS AFTER THE DEAL

This example shows the five players' hands after the third card has been dealt. The first two cards are dealt face down.

CALAMITY

JESSE

WILD BILL

DOC

ANNIE

THE BRING-IN

Once again, we shall play through a hand with our friends to see how the game functions, picking out a few pointers along the way to help you understand the basics.

Calamity is the dealer and the game is a $5/$10 fixed-limit affair with the antes set at $1 each, bets and raises in the first two rounds set at a maximum of $5, and the last three rounds requiring bets in $10 increments. After the players have received their first three cards, Calamity has to make a compulsory bet, known as the "bring-in," by virtue of having the lowest card showing. This is a nominal wager, set on this occasion at $2. Should two or more players have the same value low card, then the suits come into play alphabetically, with clubs lower than diamonds, diamonds lower than hearts, and hearts lower than spades. Determining the bring-in like this is the only time in poker that the suits have any rank.

OPENING BETS

After Calamity has bet, Jesse can fold, call the $2, or raise the betting to the $5 maximum allowed at this stage, but he cannot check. His A is good but his other cards are weak and Annie has an A face up. He calls for $2. Wild Bill has a 10 in the hole and a 10 on the board giving him a pair. He decides to advertise some strength in his hand with a $5 bet, hoping to rid the game of those with drawing hands and give his pair every chance of winning. Doc has no pair but wants to stay in the game so makes a call of $5.

Annie thinks that Wild Bill may have paired the 10 and that her overcards of an A, plus the Q that the others cannot see, might help her later so she calls as well. Calamity folds a weak hand, forfeiting just $2, and Jesse decides to do the same. This concludes the betting for the round with $24 in the pot. When folding, players should ensure their up cards are turned face down, indicating that they are no longer participating in the hand. It follows that remembering which cards have already been exposed and folded during play is important as this knowledge can influence your decisions later in the game.

After the fourth card has been dealt, the first player to bet is the one with the best visible hand, in this case Annie with her A high. Still without a pair, she checks to see if Wild Bill follows up his bet of the previous round. This he does with another $5, although he is now wondering if Annie may be slow-playing a pair of As. For Doc, with no pair and only an outside chance of improving his hand, the best advice here is to fold before the betting starts to escalate. But he calls for the $5, as does Annie.

ANNIE

WILD BILL

DOC

FIFTH STREET

Fifth street brings Wild Bill a pair of 6s to go with his 10s, while Doc and Annie each manage to pair one of their hole cards. Wild Bill has the highest visible hand and bets $10, confident that his two pairs are winning. Though he doesn't know it, he is also the only player with a possible flush draw as he possesses three cards of one suit—diamonds—with two more to come. Doc suspects he needs some help to overcome Wild Bill but he's an optimist and thinks a J might just be enough to give him two better pairs. He calls. Similarly, Annie realizes that Wild Bill bet on his 10 and thinks that her A and Q could yet help her out, so she calls the $10 as well. The pot is $69.

WILD BILL

DOC

ANNIE

SIXTH STREET

Sixth street brings no real help to anyone and Wild Bill, acting first again, bets another $10. Doc folds as he feels that while a J for two pair and an 8 for three of a kind may prove enough to win, he needs any one of five cards from the 36 he hasn't yet seen to hit. And it may still not be enough if Wild Bill already has a full house. Annie calls, though, and the final card is then dealt, face down.

WILD BILL

DOC

ANNIE

THE SHOWDOWN

The remaining two players now have their full seven cards. Wild Bill has two pair: 10s and 6s, with a 7 kicker. Annie has improved to two pair but, with only 9s and 2s plus an A kicker, she is losing. Wild Bill bets $10 and Annie, sensing that only a bluff can possibly give her a chance to win, raises another $10. Wild Bill calls and the showdown reveals that his hand is the winner, allowing him to claim a pot of $129.

This example has shown the basic mechanics of Seven-Card Stud, the dynamics of which make it an exciting and therefore popular game. Beginners are advised to play for low stakes until they develop a feel for the game and build their confidence. It is also worthwhile studying the wealth of information that exists, in print and online, to help you improve your strategic knowledge and thinking.

PROTECTING A PAIR

In fixed-limit games, like the example here, it is usual for betting to stay at the lower limit for the first two betting rounds before being raised to the upper limit on fifth street. However, if fourth street provides a player with an "open pair," (a pair visible to all players), then any player still in the hand can bet at the upper limit. In this situation, you can "protect the pair" by upping the stakes and forcing anyone hoping to draw more cards for a straight or flush to pay for the privilege. As the betting is set to increase when the fifth card is dealt, the upper limit applies for the rest of the hand.

WILD BILL

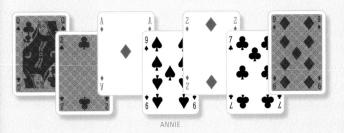

ANNIE

OMAHA HIGH

Omaha Hold 'Em or Omaha High is relative freshman on the poker scene, an there are few references to the game pric to the 1980s. Essentially it is a variation o the theme of Texas Hold 'Em, to which it ha many similarities. Omaha Hold 'Em is common referred to as Omaha High to distinguish it fror its cousin, Omaha/8, which is a high-low spli pot variation that is immensely popular i casinos and online. We will look at Omaha/ on page 112. First, though, we will concentrat on running through the basic pattern of pla for Omaha High.

To start the game, players receive four cards each, face down, from the dealer. These are their 'hole' cards. Following this there is a betting round. The game then proceeds as in Texas Hold 'Em, with the flop of three community cards being dealt face up before the next betting round. A fourth community card is then revealed prior to another betting round, and then a fifth card is turned face up. After this comes the final betting round.

BETTING STRUCTURE

The betting structure for Omaha is the same as in Texas Hold 'Em, with the two players immediately to the dealer's left required to post a small blind and a big blind. It's advisable for novices to play low-stakes fixed-limit games until they become more experienced. In tournaments and some casinos, pot-limit rules are the norm and that can make learning an expensive business.

LEGITIMATE OMAHA HANDS

Imagine having the A clubs, A diamonds, A spades, and K hearts as your hole cards (*see page 107*). A no stage will you be able to emplo all three of these As to make a han in Omaha since you can only use two of your hole cards. If the boar reads J diamonds, J hearts, K spade on the flop, Q clubs on fourth street, and 10 clubs on the river, th best you can do is make a straight The Q, J, 10 on the board matche with A, K from your hand are the cards that count. The next best hand would be two pair using two As from your hole cards and the pair of Js plus a K kicker from the board. The apparent full house opportunities of As and Ks (four hole cards and one from the board or As and Js (three from the hole and two from the board) are not legitimate hands.

HOLE CARDS

BOARD CARDS · FOURTH STREET · RIVER CARD

VALID COMBINATION
Straight—the best hand available is the Ace-high straight

HOLE CARDS

BOARD CARDS

INVALID COMBINATION
Full house—Aces over Kings is not permitted as it uses four hole cards, and one board card

HOLE CARDS

BOARD CARD

THE BASICS

Each player remaining in Omaha high to the showdown has nine cards from which to make the best poker hand: four in the hand and five face up on the table. The crucial thing about Omaha is that the player must always use two of his hole cards and three from the board to make a five-card hand. This restriction helps generate uncertainty in the game as it develops, and that inspires players to bet. With so many combinations available, the fortunes of your hand can fluctuate to a considerable degree.

AFTER THE FLOP

To help you understand Omaha, let's look at a sample hand from our friends once more, concentrating on the cards and the possibilities available to each player. We join the game after the flop when all five players can see seven of their potential nine cards from which to make a poker hand.

Wild Bill's 9 8 suited matched with the 7 10 on the flop gives him an open-ended straight draw. Any J or a 6 will make a straight while a Q J hearts or J 7 hearts will give him a straight flush. However, if the Q J hearts did come up on fourth street and the river, he may run into somebody holding A K hearts, giving them an unbeatable royal flush. Doc has little going for him with no pairs, an outside chance of a low flush in clubs, and a low straight draw.

Annie has made a pair of Ks and also has the same straight draw chances as Wild Bill with her 9 8 suited. The K spades on the flop also provides her with a flush possibility. As with Texas Hold 'Em, unless there are at least three cards of one suit amongst the community cards, a flush is not possible.

Calamity has a poor hand with only a pair of 3s in the hole and no help from the flop, added to which she cannot make a straight or a flush given the cards available to her. Her only chance to win would come if the other two 3s appear on fourth street and the river, and that's unlikely. Similarly, Jesse's pair of 2s is weak, but he does at least have an Ace-high flush draw available to him, should he wish to gamble.

> ### GOOD STARTING HANDS
> ——— ◆ ———
>
> In Omaha, gauging the strength of your opening hand of four cards is as crucial as in any poker variation. Any two of your hole cards could turn out to be winners, but which two? Having a pair in your hand is good, the higher the better. Having two connecting cards or two suited cards is also helpful.
>
> Satisfying all these combinations among your hole cards is ideal as you can improve a pair to three or four of a kind, or a full house, and still have chances of flush and straight draws.

WILD BILL

DOC

ANNIE

CALAMITY

JESSE

THE FLOP

FOURTH STREET

Fourth street brings a J spades, which provides both Wild
Bill and Annie with identical straights, using the 9 8 in
their hand with the 7 10 J on the board. Should the river
card be a Q, Wild Bill can improve his straight to Q J 10 9 8, but
Annie would beat him, since she could then use the K 9 in her hand with
the 10 J Q to make a better straight. Remember, Wild Bill cannot make an
Ace-high straight because to do so would mean using only the A from his
hole cards with four from the board.

Annie can improve to a flush if the river card is a spade, but Jesse would
be in pole position in this eventuality since he also has two spades in his
hand, including the A.

BOARD CARDS

FOURTH STREET

BETTING STRATEGY
◆

Omaha High is sometimes regarded as a game of straights and
flushes, with the opportunities to hit them improved by having
four hole cards at the outset. Therefore, if you are sitting on a
pair and the board helps you improve to three of a kind, you
will want to bet aggressively to persuade opponents to give
up straight and flush draws. Of course, this is a tactic
that works best with higher betting limits, as is the
case in virtually all poker games. Trying to play
cute, by allowing others to swell the pot and see
more cards, can backfire if there are several
players still in at the showdown. If your three
of a kind doesn't improve to a full house,
somebody may well overtake you and you'll
have to sit and watch while they win the pot.

> You boys from Omaha sure don't know how to treat a lady!

THE RIVER

As it is, the river card is another K, giving Annie three Ks, which is no improvement on her straight and leaves her tied with Wild Bill. Of course, without dwelling on any betting patterns here, a showdown between all the players would leave Wild Bill and Annie sharing the pot with the best hand, a Jack-high straight. But if Annie had raised the betting after the flop with the top pair, a flush draw, and a straight draw, she may have frightened the others away and won the pot then. Even when the J appeared on fourth street to tie her hand with Wild Bill's, her flush draw in spades would have given her a slight edge, especially as it would outdraw anyone who had an A Q in their hand, giving them the high straight.

FOURTH STREET

RIVER CARD

OMAHA/8

Omaha/8, an abbreviation of Omaha Hol
'Em 8-or-Better High-Low Split Poker,
another variation that is growing i
popularity within the poker communit
For novices still grappling with the concepts c
Texas Hold 'Em and Omaha High, this is a gam
that may be best left until you are confident i
your strategic play. Plenty of online card room
offer Omaha/8 among their range of games s
the chance exists to gain plenty of practice.

The structure of the game is the same as for Omaha Hig
with players each receiving four cards face down and the tw
players to the dealer's left posting the small and big blinds
initiate betting before the flop. Subsequent betting roun
occur after the flop, the turn, and the river cards are expose
To win, a player must use two of his hole cards with thr
cards from the board to make either the highest or lowe
hand. The pot is divided equally between the two and, ideal
players want to win both hands.

BELOW
Omaha/8 is a high-low split pot game. That's two shots at the money but be sure you know what you're doing.

You know, I think you'll like Omaha/8. The best hand wins; the worst hand wins. How can you lose?

PLAY

PASS

STARTING HANDS

Yes, you've guessed it. Judging your hole cards before deciding whether to enter the hand is crucial to successful Omaha/8 play. Having four cards provides you with six different two-card combinations that could tempt the unwary into seeing winning opportunities all round. But this is rarely the case. A hand such as K clubs, K hearts, 10 spades, 9 diamonds leaves you no scope for hitting a low hand, meaning that you are forced to play high. If the flop is 6 clubs, 5 clubs, 3 clubs, then your attractive pair of Ks immediately looks vulnerable to any straight or flush for the high hand. You could already be "drawing dead," meaning there is no chance of you beating a hand already made by an opponent.

OBJECT OF THE GAME

As Omaha/8 is a split-pot game, both the highest and the lowest hands will share the pot equally, unless there is no qualifying low hand. In this case, the high hand takes the lot. Betting strongly for one or other eventuality is fine provided your cards are clearly defining which angle you should play. Ideally, however, "scooping the pot" is the aim and you should be playing hands that give you every opportunity of winning both high and low.

LEGITIMATE HANDS

The possibility of winning both halves of the pot comes from players being able to combine any cards to make a high and low hand, provided they meet the requirement of two from the hole and three from the board. But, to qualify for a chance at the low-hand payout, the five cards must include no pair and be ranked in value at 8 or lower. For example, 8, 7, 5, 4, 2 is a legitimate low hand while 6, 5, 4, 2, 2 will not count because of the pair of 2s.

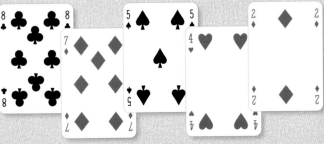

LEGITIMATE HAND

INVALID LOW HAND

SCOOPS

Players are not obliged to specify whether they are betting for the high or low share of the pot and it is possible to "scoop" the entire pot by using the same hand for both high and low. A straight flush of 5, 4, 3, 2, A diamonds could well be the highest hand in a game and yet, because As can count low too, it counts as the perfect low hand simultaneously. Straights and flushes, as is typical in split-pot and lowball poker generally, do not feature in the low game spectrum.

Should no low hand qualify for a share, the high hand wins the entire pot.

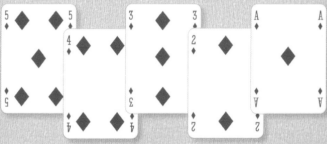

STRAIGHT FLUSH

PLAYING THE FLOP

Discipline is crucial when playing poker. This particularly applies to Omaha/8, where players are often involved in too many hands because of the apparent possibilities that emerge. If you are in at the flop, you will be able to see seven of your possible nine cards and should be calculating the number of "outs" available to you—that is, the cards left in the deck that can put you in a winning position. If you detect that you have a favorable chance of hitting the best possible hand, bet accordingly. Experienced Omaha/8 players consider the game purely in terms of probability, betting to advertise the odds are in their favor and rarely contemplating a bluff.

SIMPLE STRATEGIES

Remember, there is always a winning high hand but not always a qualifier for best low hand. If you have high-value cards in the hole and the flop fits, bet to make it costly for anyone to draw low for a share of the pot. If the flop is entirely composed of high cards, the chances are everyone is playing for the high end anyway. Monitoring the action will also help you to avoid the risk of "quartering" the pot. This is what happens when you hit an identical high or low hand to that of an opponent and you end up splitting your half share of the pot in half again. It doesn't help your mood or your chip stack.

SEVEN-CARD STUD/8

Seven-Card Stud 8-or-Better High-Low Split Poker, or Seven-Card Stud/8 for short, is played in the same fashion as its high-only forebear. The pot is split equally between the best high and best low hands, with players aiming for high, low or both using any combination of five cards from their allotted seven. To qualify for a low hand, players must have five unpaired cards ranked 8 or lower, otherwise the whole pot will automatically go to the high hand.

The popularity of the game is increasing and, as with some of the other poker derivations, this has much to do with the potential for speedily inflated pots. The lure of winning at least half the pot with a brilliantly high or unbeatable low hand encourages players to continue in a game when, perhaps, they ought to have folded earlier. But that just means more chips for the winners. Scooping the pot with the best high and low hands should be every player's prime objective.

BELOW
Sometimes in split-pot games it pays to be the only player aiming high—or low, of course.

ABOVE
After the deal,
the player with the lowest
"up card" brings in the
betting by acting first.

Beginning the game usually involves everyone putting in the ante before the deal, two cards face down and one face up to each player, after which the lowest exposed card brings in the betting. As further cards are dealt, from fourth street onward it is the highest visible card that bets first, as usual.

If play continues to a showdown, there is no need for contenders to declare whether they are playing high or low. The result is determined by "letting the cards speak," which simply means that the division of the spoils is adjudged by the value of the hands themselves. Of course, away from organized card rooms and casinos, players may decide that a declaration is perfectly acceptable. In this case, a player declaring high and low will probably have to succeed both ways to claim the pot or forfeit any claim to the pot at all. Winning one way would not be acceptable.

There is one other aspect of play that differs slightly from the high-only version of the game. Protecting a pair by betting at the higher limit in fixed-limit games (*see page 105*) is not allowed.

(*see page 105*)

STRATEGY

The more complex a poker game you play, the more you have to concentrate in order to succeed. Most experts recommend patience when playing this variation, preferring to wait for a playable hand of cards that work together rather than betting speculatively at the outset. Observing folded cards and calculating potential outs is important in Seven-Card Stud/8, but betting patterns and exposed cards offer clues, too. If you are looking at a low draw and figure that all but one of your opponents is doing likewise, the best you may expect is to split half the pot. This may be a poor return on your investment. The player with the high hand, of course, has a clear run at half the pot and would be delighted to see others stoking it up while squabbling over the low hand. Balanced against this is the frustration that comes from having a premium high hand yet still only winning half the chips. And that brings us back to being patient and disciplined.

HIGH AND LOW HAND
POSSIBILITIES

STARTING HANDS
◆

Low hands are always good, particularly if you have suited cards and As in the hole. A hand consisting only of high cards can realistically go in just one direction but will win the entire pot if there is no qualified low hand. With, say, half-a-dozen players at the table, a low hand is probably out there. A low hand with the potential to develop into a straight or a potent flush presents more opportunities. Something like A hearts, 7 hearts, 5 hearts is ideal with three cards lower than an 8 and all of them suited. At the other end of the scale, K spades, Q spades, J spades leaves you little room to maneuver. Going high is the only direction open to you, but supporting this move too vigorously could lead to a string of medium or low cards appearing, thus ruining your chances both ways.

HIGH HAND CHANCES ONLY

DIRECTION

Determining the "direction" in which a player is going, either high or low, is crucial. In studying your opponents' play for clues, both from their exposed cards and their betting patterns, you may gain a tactical edge. For example, *see below*, if a player has 2 hearts, 4 spades, 5 clubs showing after fifth street, the odds are that they are aiming low. Alternatively, a K hearts, K clubs, Q hearts on display advertises a player's likely direction quite clearly. Of course, the same information is available to your opponents in looking at your exposed cards. So, being able to disguise a hand is an advantage and an A in the hole is always comforting.

BELOW
These examples show how a player's direction might be determined from the visible cards.

EXAMPLE 1

EXAMPLE 2

LOWBALL

Lowball is a popular variation played in the same fashion as classic Five-Card Draw Poker. As such, players are dealt five cards face down before the first betting round, then they draw replacement cards as required and conduct the second, and final, betting round. The difference, as the name suggests, is that players are trying to win with the lowest hand possible rather than the highest.

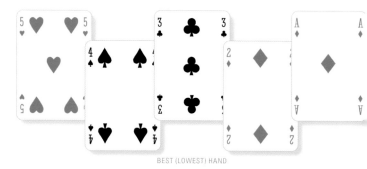

BEST (LOWEST) HAND

This leads to a modification in the ranking of hands with straights and flushes discounted altogether and As always counting low. The best (i.e. lowest) hand is 5, 4, 3, 2, A, which is known as a "wheel" or "bicycle." As straights, flushes, and in this instance, even straight flushes, are ignored, this hand represents the lowest five cards, unpaired, that it is possible to hold. The next lowest hand is 6, 4, 3, 2, A, which beats 6, 5, 3, 2, A since, with the high cards being of identical value, the next highest counts and 4 is lower than 5.

Because of the complete change in perspective when judging a hand, Lowball can take a while to work out. But the game becomes easier with experience, and even novice players will learn quite quickly that a handful of picture cards should probably be folded at the earliest opportunity.

2ND LOWEST HAND

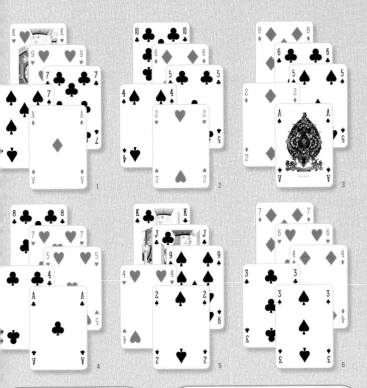

LOWBALL OPPORTUNITY

Though it is declining in popularity, the traditional Draw Poker game historically requires players to open the betting with at least a pair of Js in their hand. If everyone has bet an ante but nobody has a sufficiently good hand to open the betting proper, the cards are normally folded and players ante-up once more ready for a fresh game. Rather than do that, some players prefer to play a hand of Lowball instead, since, with nobody possessing better than a medium pair, low hands are obviously prevalent.

PLAYABLE HANDS

When you are used to searching for the highest hand in poker, switching your thinking to accommodate Lowball can take a moment or two. What must be remembered is that even a low pair such as 2s or 3s is likely to be too strong a hand to win at Lowball if there are several players in the game. Consequently, playing pat hands or hands requiring a one-card draw is often the best policy. Drawing two or more replacements simply presents the likelihood of hitting damaging high cards and pairs.

ABOVE
All these examples represent poor hands in normal poker, but much better Lowball hands. Hand 3 wins this Lowball showdown, and the hands rank in descending order: 3, 4, 2, 5, 6, 1.

CRISSCROSS OR IRON CROSS

his is a stimulating game that car theoretically, accommodate up to nin players in a hand. Five cards are dealt fac down to each player and a further fiv cards are placed face down on the board to form . cross. Each player normally makes a nominal be for the ante and betting proper begins when th first of the board cards is exposed. These ar turned face up in a clockwise fashion, with th central card exposed last. After each card in th cross is revealed, a betting round follows, makin five betting rounds in total.

The object of the game is to make the best poker hand usin only two cards from your starting hand with three from eithe the vertical or horizontal line of the cross. This restrictio means that winning hands can be quite low, with two pairs c three of a kind proving to be strong. But straights, flushe or better are perfectly feasible. With five betting rounds staying involved to the showdown can prove expensive if th stakes are high.

A look at an example played out by our buddies shoul help you grasp the basic principles of the game. Calamity the dealer, and we approach the game after the fourth bettin round with all the board cards exposed except for the one i the center of the cross.

Working around the table, Jesse's best potential hand is 5-high straight using the 2 3 in his hand with the vertical lin of 5 4 A, provided the central card is a 4. It will be apparen that a flush is only feasible if there is a line of cards all of on suit, while, for a straight, closely matched or consecutive card are necessary.

Jesse also has the possibility of hitting three 2s should th central card be a 2, giving him a hand of 2 2 2 K 8 via th horizontal line. Wild Bill has exactly the same possibilitie open to him at this stage. Doc has three of a kind as his bes potential hand, needing a 5 in the center to give him 5 5 A o the board with a 5 and K from his hole cards.

Annie and Calamity have similar possibilities for three of kind, too. An A would give Annie A A A Q 5 on the vertica line, and an 8 offers her 8 8 8 A 2 on the horizontal

Calamity would be losing to Annie should an A appear because her best hand would be A A A J 5, reinforcing the importance of the kickers. However, a J in the center would provide her with J J J 8 2 and that would be enough to win the pot.

As it happens, the final card to be exposed is the 8 clubs, giving Annie the strongest hand. However, bear in mind that, in this example, the sequence of cards revealed is 5 diamonds, 2 clubs, A hearts, 8 spades, and finally 8 clubs in the center. In a vigorous betting heat for large stakes, would Annie have hung on long enough to remain in the pot? Aggressive betting, as ever, could keep potential winning hands out of the action.

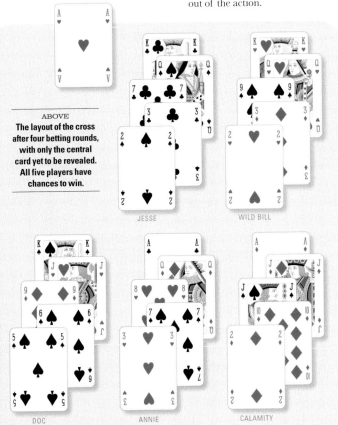

ABOVE
The layout of the cross after four betting rounds, with only the central card yet to be revealed. All five players have chances to win.

JESSE WILD BILL

DOC ANNIE CALAMITY

PINEAPPLE AND CRAZY PINEAPPLE

Pineapple and the more widely played Crazy Pineapple are variations on the Texas Hold 'Em theme. The pattern of play is the same as in Hold 'Em except that each player is dealt three cards face down, instead of two, to begin the game. In Pineapple, players must discard one of their three hole cards *before* the flop, while in Crazy Pineapple, the discard is jettisoned *after* the flop, usually when the betting round at that stage is complete.

STRATEGY

Crazy Pineapple presents an interesting strategic proposition. Sometimes you may wish to discard a card that is already part of a good hand because a better opportunity exists. For example, say you have K hearts, J spades, and 10 hearts in your hand and the flop is Q hearts, J diamonds, and J hearts. If you retain the J and the K, then you have three of a kind and the possibility of improving to at least a full house and maybe four Js. But not many cards help you, and if a Q arrives on fourth street, your full house would be inferior to anyone holding another Q.

Alternatively, keeping the K, 10 hearts opens up straight possibilities with any A or 9, straight flush possibilities if either of these is a heart, and flush possibilities with the remaining seven hearts in the deck. All these are superior holdings to three Js, though that may still be strong enough to win the pot. But, in a many-handed game, with those extra cards circulating before the flop, you'll be looking at chances like this to improve your hand.

The benefit to players in Crazy Pineapple is that they have more information available to them when deciding which card to throw away, no doubt a contributory factor to it being the preferred version. It provides scope for apparently poor hole cards to develop into winners, thus encouraging more players to stay in the game rather than folding before the flop.

STARTING HANDS

As in Hold 'Em, being dealt a high pair or suited connectors is obviously good. Of course, if you are dealt three As, one of them will have to be discarded but, painful though that may be, at least you are aware that only one other A remains in the game, knowledge that your opponents do not possess. In general, a good starting hand is going to correspond with those that can be viably played in Hold 'Em.

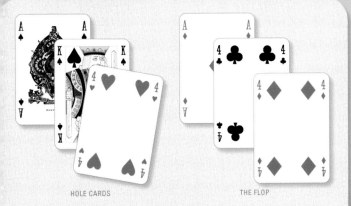

HOLE CARDS   THE FLOP

◆ PINEAPPLE ◆

To illustrate the difference between the two versions, let's consider this example. Say you were dealt A spades, K spades, and 4 hearts. You'd be happy to play the A K suited in Hold 'Em so, playing Pineapple, you'd most likely discard the 4. If the flop missed your hand completely, you'd probably fold and wait for the next deal. To see A 4 4 on the flop would be excruciating, even though you'd still have two pair and top kicker.

◆ CRAZY PINEAPPLE ◆

See the same hand in Crazy Pineapple, of course, and a flop of A 4 4 will have you discarding the K in no time. The full house of 4s over As would have to be worth supporting since only someone with the other two As could be ahead of you. That would be nothing short of miraculous.

And if that doesn't sound challenging enough, Crazy Pineapple is often played as a high-low, split-pot game!

ENGLISH SEVEN-CARD STUD

Another variation on a theme, English Seven-Card Stud deviates from the standard game of Seven-Card Stud (*see page 100*) after fifth street. Remember players still in the game will have their two hole cards face down, and three further cards face up. Once betting is concluded on fifth street, players may discard one card and be dealt another. A face-down card that is discarded is replaced with another down card, while a face-up card is, naturally, replaced with another dealt face up.

Now another betting round takes place, after which those players still in the game once again have the option to replace an up card or a down card. The final round of betting then takes place, with a showdown resulting if more than one player is still contesting the pot. At this point in the game competing players will have five cards: two face down and three face up.

An important point to bear in mind is that a player who decides to stand pat with their original five cards when offered the chance to exchange must play those cards to the conclusion of the hand. They cannot retain their hand at the first exchange opportunity and then, before the final betting round, decide to reject a card in favor of another dealt from the deck.

RIGHT
When playing Seven-Card Stud in England, remember that it's never too late to change your mind—or your hand!

London

PLAYER 1

after fifth street

after first card exchange

PLAYER 2

after fifth street

after first card exchange

PLAYER 3

after fifth street

after first card exchange

PLAYER 4

after fifth street

after first card exchange

OPTIONS

After betting is concluded on fifth street, the players each have the chance to change one card. An up card is always replaced with another up card, and a down card with a down card. Player 1 has replaced a down card, players 2, 3 and 4 have replaced an up card. There will now be a round of betting, followed by another chance to change a card, and then a final round of betting.

MEXICAN STUD

This is a variation of Five-Card Stud, although it can be played with more cards depending on the number of betting rounds that players decide is appropriate. Each player is dealt two cards face down. Then, having looked at their hole cards, each player selects one to be exposed face up. This is done simultaneously so that nobody has a chance to change their selection based on cards that have already been exposed.

A betting round follows before a third card is dealt face down to each remaining player. Now players decide whether to expose this card or their hole card, again revealing their choice simultaneously.

This pattern is repeated with a betting round after every card is dealt until, in a five-card example, players continuing to a showdown have one card face down and their other four cards face up.

MEXICAN STUD STRATEGY
◆

Unless dealt a pair in the first two cards, most players will reveal the lower of their opening two cards to disguise the value of their hand, though this is obviously not compulsory. As the game progresses, players are not obliged to indicate whether each card they expose is the latest they've been dealt or their original hole card. This helps sustain the air of uncertainty during proceedings and improves the chances of bluffing, which is tricky with so much of your hand exposed.

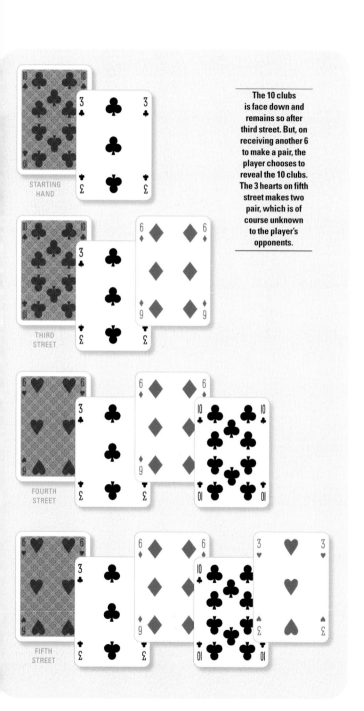

STARTING
HAND

THIRD
STREET

FOURTH
STREET

FIFTH
STREET

The 10 clubs is face down and remains so after third street. But, on receiving another 6 to make a pair, the player chooses to reveal the 10 clubs. The 3 hearts on fifth street makes two pair, which is of course unknown to the player's opponents.

RAZZ

RIGHT
The highest up card begins the betting. If two players have the same value card—Qs, for example—then the suits come in to play, with spades highest.

Razz is simply Seven-Card Stud Lowball, played in the same way as Seven-Card Stud but with the lowest hand winning the pot. Once again, straights and flushes do not count so the best hand, even if it's all suited, is a wheel, namely 5, 4, 3, 2, A.

Another slight difference is in the betting action, with th[e] highest exposed card after the deal "bringing in" the actio[n] rather than the lowest, as in Seven-Card Stud. If two playe[rs] share the same value high card, then the suits are used [to] determine who bets first, with spades ranking highest followe[d] by hearts, diamonds, and clubs. So, in opening the betting, [a] player with a Q spades is considered to have a higher car[d] than a player holding a Q hearts.

On subsequent betting rounds from fourth stre[et] onward, the lowest hand, not the highest, starts th[e] betting. If two players have identical low hands, it is th[e] player nearest the dealer's left who bets first i[n] that round. One other thing to note is th[e] question of protecting the pair (*see page 105*) which is a legitimate tactic in regula[r] Seven-Card Stud with fixed bettin[g] limits. This is ignored in Razz as a visib[le] pair is likely to have yo[u] struggling to win the pot an[d] is hardly worth protecting.

BELOW
Common to most Lowball games is th[e] fact that straights ar[e] flushes are not counted. So, in Raz[z] the lowest hand is [a] "wheel"—a straigh[t] of 5, 4, 3, 2, A.

In Razz, player 1 would open the betting because the Q spades is ranked higher, and therefore worse, than player 4's Q hearts.

PLAYER 1
The Q spades is the highest card showing, but the A 2 in the hole is promising.

PLAYER 2
Hole cards of 5 6 suited are low. A pair of 5s are not necessarily a problem because the player can discount one of them in the final hand.

PLAYER 3
Unlucky to find a pair of 9s in the hole. This hand needs too many low cards.

PLAYER 4
As the lowest hand triumphs in Razz, holding any cards higher than a 7 will cause problems.

PLAYER 5
A pair of 3s is not disastrous since player 5 can discount one of them in his final hand.

CHICAGO AND BLACK MARIAH

A nother variation on the theme of Seven-Card Stud is Chicago, also sometimes called High Chicago, with the object being to make the highest poker hand from your seven available cards. The pot is split between the player with the best hand and any player who has the highest spade as a hole card. If no player has a spade among his hole cards, then the best hand claims the whole pot. It follows that, if you possess an A spades among your hole cards, you are guaranteed half the pot.

Black Mariah is an almost identical game with one important difference. To win the pot a player must have the best hand and possess the highest spade of the hole cards. If this is not the case, then the pot remains in place and everybody bets an ante once more and a new hand is dealt. Obviously, this is a method of inflating pots to retain everybody's interest and, again, if dealt the A spades as a hole card, a player can exert betting pressure in the hope of knocking all his opponents out and claiming the whole prize to himself.

BELOW
If you're playing poker in Chicago, a A spades in the hol should leave your opponents with a severe case of the blues.

PLAYER 1
Without the K spades in the hole, this full house of Ks over Qs is not quite as strong as it seems.

Playing Chicago, player 1's full house of Ks over Qs is the higher hand, but player 2 has the A spades in the hold and can claim half the pot. In Black Mariah, neither player would be able to claim the pot, because the winner must have the best hand and the highest spade in the hole.

PLAYER 2
Having the A spades represents insurance for player 2 in either Chicago or Black Mariah.

MIDNIGHT BASEBALL

idnight Baseball is an appealing an generally light-hearted game that tests player's judgement in making a hanc although the nature of the game preclude bluffing. The use of wild cards adds an excitin twist to poker games.

Antes are optional, and each player is dealt seven cards fac down with nobody permitted to look at their hands durin play. The player on the dealer's left then turns his top car face up with this exposed card representing the best hand i play at that moment. He can check, bet or fold. If he bet other players have to call—or raise, of course—to stay in th game. When the betting is concluded for the round, the nex player to the left still remaining in the game turns his top car face up. Should the exposed card be lower than that c player 1, he must continue to reveal his carc one at a time until the hand showing is enoug to take the lead. It is then his turn to decid whether to check, bet, or fold.

Play continues in this fashion around th table, with each player in succession having t improve on the best visible hand befor making a betting decision. When a player ha exposed all his cards yet is still behinc he is out of the game. The winner is th player with the best hand showing whe everyone has either exposed all their cards c already folded.

WILD CARDS
◆

In Midnight Baseball, all 3s and 9s are wild cards and if a player reveals a 4, he has the option of being dealt an extra card, face up, from the top of the deck. If exercising this option, he can expect to pay a nominal fee into the pot. Unlike 3s and 9s, 4s are only worth their face value.

PLAYER 1

PLAYER 2

PLAYER 3

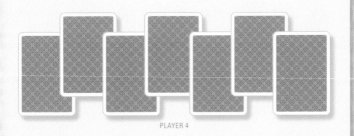

PLAYER 4

SHOTGUN POKER

This game is a variation of Draw Poker that involves extra betting rounds to prolong the hand and swell the pot. Players receive just three cards at first, face down, at which point there is a betting round. Those players remaining in the game then receive a fourth card followed by another betting round. After the fifth card is dealt, the game proceeds in the same fashion as Draw Poker, with a betting round, the draw, and then a final round of betting before any potential showdown.

PLAYER 1

PLAYER 2

PLAYER 3

PLAYER 4

In Shotgun Poker, the first betting round occurs after each player has been dealt just three cards. At this stage of the game, there are still four rounds of betting to come, so you should be sure you want to remain in the game. In this example, players 1 and 3 may be feeling confident, but both could find themselves totally outgunned if player 4 is able to develop his three 9s into a winning hand.

INDIAN POKER

> I can't see an Ace or a King: a Queen might just win this...

A simple game that, despite its name, is not really a poker variation at all, although it can be a bit of fun. Players are dealt one card face down which, without looking at it, they then hold to their forehead so it is exposed for all other players to see. Betting starts with the player to the dealer's left, as usual, and continues until all but one player has folded or there is a showdown. The fun comes from watching timid players fold high cards in the face of strong betting while others are prepared to bet blind on a lowly 2 all the way to the end.

ABOVE
Before betting, each player holds his card to his forehead. Therefore, every hand is visible to him except his own.

GAME STRATEGIES

ince this is a book primarily for beginners, in this chapter we shall consider how to establish a game and how best to conduct yourself during play. Although we shall take a brief look at the strategies and tactics that apply in card rooms, casinos, and tournaments, the main focus of attention will be the home game. This, after all, is where poker maintains its hold on the public imagination since this is where most poker games are played.

The chapter on Poker Basics gave some pointers on friendly games while indicating that organization, clearly stated rules, and a courteous outlook are all important to a successful poker session. Here we shall explore some of those points in greater detail to illustrate the potential traps that await the poorly prepared player.

Also, since it is as much a part of the home poker scene as inviting round a few competitive friends for a game, we'll consider some strategies to be applied when playing online poker. For those who wish to learn more about the experience, consult the chapter, Where to Play (*see page 176*), which includes a detailed outline of what to expect from an online card room.

RIGHT
Online poker is booming and reinforcing the popularity of the game. However, there are times when playing an opponent face to face can have its reward.

PLANNING A GAME

Assuming you've heard a few friends talking about poker and perhaps, read a few articles on the growing popularity of the game, you will probably be eager to get your hands dirty playing some cards. That's all fine and dandy, but where do you find a game? Yes, a trip to the casino could be a place to start, but you can be sure that, as a beginner, you will be targeted by experienced players eager to relieve you of your bankroll. If that happens too often, believe me your enthusiasm for the game could soon fade.

Playing online is a possibility, but only if you have access to the required technology. While it is a good place to practice what you've learned so far, the action is quick and it can take a little time to become familiar with the format of the games. So, do any of your buddies play poker or, perhaps more to the point, do you know some people who are as eager to learn about the game as you are? If so, then you need to get organized.

All social activity needs someone to instigate a plan and others to back it up, however informal the event. Poker games are no different. Let's say that you, personally, are an enthusiastic individual with a spare evening or two each week that you are keen to fill. A poker school is just one option, but are you and your card-playing friends able to commit yourselves to a regular session each week, or each month? The more you play, the more experienced you become and, in time, more skilled as well. But there's nothing more frustrating than looking forward to a game only to find that everybody else has forgotten about it or found something else to do.

So the first requirement is to agree on a regular time and a venue for the game. The player who has the greatest tendency toward organization, should make a point of ensuring that other members of the school are informed of the time and place of the next game.

ABOVE
When considering a game, think about the size of your bankroll. Play for stakes that suit your pocket.

POKER CHIPS

There's simply no doubt that using proper poker chips brings credibility to a game. Apart from being cleaner and easier to use than cash, they help speed up the action. The best are made of clay or, as is more likely these days, some durable composite material that gives them a bit of weight. The colors, indicating the denominations, vary depending on the manufacturer, but the following is a traditional guide to chip values.

$1	White
$5	Red
$25	Green
$100	Black
$500	Purple

Providing a deck of cards, chips, food, and drink should be the responsibility of all, but most card schools have someone who will ensure that all these aspects are covered. I've participated in a regular game where the driving force behind it often plays host, galvanizes the rest of us into turning up and also bakes home-made pizza. Crucially, he likes to entertain guests with tales of misbehaving celebrities and bad jokes, which makes it easy for the rest of us to agree to come again.

As you will gather, this particular game is a light-hearted affair with the emphasis on fun rather than serious play. That is the next aspect to consider when organizing a poker school. Just how serious is the game? To an extent, it will be reflected in the level of the stakes for which you want to play. Without referring to any specific sums, it's best to play with a bankroll that will hurt you if you lose it, but will not leave you short of the rent or something to eat. Whether that figure is $20 or $20,000 is immaterial, just find the stake level that suits you. Play will be more meaningful and the knowledge that you are in no danger of bankruptcy will help you to express yourself in your poker play. And that's important.

Competitiveness is the driving force behind poker; that's what makes it a gambling game. But how competitive are you and your poker buddies? While you may have agreed on the bankroll required to sit in at the game, how determined are you to send a few friends home with just small change in their pockets? I've lost count of the guys I've encountered who were happy to sit in on a sociable game expecting a little "schooling," only to find themselves on the losing end of a seriously big pot. Trust me, their mood changes as they realize, all too late, that they haven't been playing seriously enough and that their "friends" are after their money. Having just lost the cab fare home, they then face the prospect of a lonely walk with nothing but a reassessment of their buddies' competitive instincts to keep them company.

Obviously you want to play poker to win, but there are aesthetic and social considerations to playing the game, too. Losing friends over poker is not cool. So, having decided on the amount required to buy in to a game, what about the betting structure? No-limit and pot-limit poker is typical in tournament play, but the chances are that few home-game players will be interested in risking their entire chip stack on one hand, especially when new to the game. Well, may be not until after the pizza has arrived and they've sunk a few beers anyway.

Fixed-limit or spread-limit games are better options with, perhaps, a raising of the levels as the session nears its designated finishing time. Do agree ahead of time on the expected duration of the game and make sure anyone thinking of leaving early has notified the other players. This prevents someone from cleaning up with a couple of big pots and then making their excuses before the others have a chance to win their money back.

ABOVE
Poker is a great excuse for a social evening. Pizza and beer are optional, of course, but a bankro is essential, even if you only have some small change.

SCHOOLING

Schooling describes the looser play expected at a table populated by poor players competing for low-level stakes. In this situation, players call more bets and stay in more pots because their judgment is questionable. Since few bluffs will work, plenty of hands are seen at the showdown and the chips keep moving around the table. The benefit of this is that players can "go to school" by observing the patterns of play and, it is hoped, learning to improve their judgment from what they see unfolding.

CHOOSING THE BETTING STRUCTURE

Poker is played with four recognizable betting structures: no-limit, pot-limit, spread-limit, and fixed-limit. Choosing the most suitable for your game is the key to an enjoyable session for all players. Tournaments favor no-limit and pot-limit poker because these provoke volatile betting exchanges and force players to take risks. Either they win big or are eliminated. Fixed-limit and spread-limit games are much more common as these help players to calculate the maximum cost of staying in any hand. This is very helpful in encouraging tentative players to tackle the game.

Provided the limits are agreed to everybody's taste, the next point to acknowledge is that these limits will affect the play during the game. The power of no-limit poker comes from the risk inherent in betting your entire stack. Such a move always commands respect, making it a handy weapon to have if contemplating a bluff, and even handier when intimidating a player with fewer chips. Imagine yourself in the position of having a moderate hand that you suspect is a loser, but being able to force an opponent to go all-in if they want to call your bluff. You have chips to spare and will stay in the game even if you lose the hand. They risk losing all their chips to satisfy their curiosity.

In fixed-limit poker for small stakes, there is a cap on the amount you can bet or raise. This makes the financial risk of calling much lower for your opponents, so bluffing in the same situation has a correspondingly higher risk. You're not going to get away with it so often.

CHOOSING A GAME

Having organized where, when, and how regularly to play, as well as who wants to be involved, the next question is: What poker variation do you choose? The basic games of Draw and Stud, plus the community card games, have been covered already as they are the most popular poker variants in town. A small selection of exotic derivations have also been briefly explained but there are literally hundreds of poker games from which to choose your favorite. Wild Kings, Follow the Queen, Pass the Trash, Death Wheel—all have their place. Selection is down to a matter of taste and, perhaps, the mood at the poker table. The willingness to play with cards is also going to be governed by the same factors. So what do you want to play?

Dealer's choice is a popular feature of home games and can introduce players to variations that, in some cases, have only a tenuous link to poker. From the strategic point of view, this is a nightmare for beginners desperately trying to come to terms with calculating out probability, and pot odds. Even for a more experienced player switching the mindset to fit one crazy variation after another can be confusing. Personally speaking, dealer choice is not a thrilling prospect, but some people believe that a true poker player takes whatever game is on offer. And I can see their point. Although gambling makes poker interesting, contemplating the ideas strategies and theories behind some weird variation is as much a part of the fun as actually scooping a pot. Sometimes, you see, it isn't enough just to win money from your opponents you have to feel that you understood the game better than the others and it was your skill that ensured you won. I think it's something to do with ego.

ABOVE
Deciding what poker game to play is crucial. Also, remember that playing with wild cards will affect the quality of hand required to win.

Choosing a game is also going to be affected by the number of players wishing to participate. Nine or ten players at the table immediately rules out draw games involving five or more cards unless you want to play with two decks, but let's not go there. Yet Texas Hold 'Em can comfortably be played with nine or ten at the table, as is customary in casinos and online. Seven-Card Stud will work with up to eight players because it is expected that enough hands will be folded during the game for the full deck of 52 cards to prove adequate. As you can see a grasp of basic math is important before you even begin to play and start calculating the likelihood of a win.

DEALER'S CHOICE

The key to dealer's choice is that no player, when dealing, should choose a game which is to their advantage in any way. As for wild card variations, well, some players feel they need all the help they can get at the table. Introducing wild cards has two telling effects on a game. First, the winning hand is likely to be higher than normal. Second, it is difficult to assess your chances of winning, especially if you have no wild cards in your hand. This increases the luck factor and reduces the level of skill required to win a pot. Whether this appeals to you or not will depend on how serious a player you are and how deeply you are attached to your chips.

BELOW
A classic image of a poker game. Honest, hardworking gentlemen gathered round a table to indulge in some friendly rivalry.

HOW MANY PLAYERS?
◆

The number of players also has an impact on your betting strategy, no matter what poker variation is played. As a general rule, the more players there are in the game, the better the winning hand will have to be. This holds true in pretty much all of the standard poker games. It follows that you can be more aggressive when playing "short-handed" games, involving three or four players, than you can when sitting at a table of up to ten players. Conservative play is then required as, potentially, a lot of good hands could be in opposition.

KNOWING YOUR OPPONENTS

It has been suggested that poker is about playing people rather than cards. This is because the game draws on our instinctive desires for status and power, while we try to ward off threat and counterthreat. Knowing the playing styles and personalities of opponents is therefore crucial to any player's success. Are they timid or aggressive? High or low on confidence? Alert or distracted? Awareness of these character traits may help when confronting someone over a big pot. Indeed, regulated confrontation is the essence of poker.

Assessing the mood and playing style of your opponents is important in selecting a game, as well as being crucial to your chances of performing to the best of your ability. If your friends are enthusiastic to play and you've known them for a while, you may already have an idea of how they might play poker, assuming they're beginners too. Once you graduate to more formal games, you'll be looking for clues to the personalities of strangers at the table, perhaps in how they talk, dress, or sit. Ideally, on entering a real card room, try to watch the game for a while to get a feel for the play, picking up any points of interest regarding the other players. Failing that, ease yourself into the game without being too bold for, as the saying goes, if you haven't spotted the sucker at the table, it must be you.

LEFT
In short-handed games you can play more aggressively. A lowly pair of 8s may be very strong against just two opponents.

CARD ROOM STRATEGY

Settling in for a game among seasoned players can be a daunting experience for the novice and isn't recommended for anyone lacking confidence in their ability to read a hand and manage their chips. Regular cash games without a time limit dictate that you should maintain a patient and disciplined approach. This doesn't exclude you from playing loosely now and again since, if you play too conservatively, rest assured it will be spotted. As a result, you may not exploit a decent hand to its full potential.

ABOVE
In card rooms, you'll find keen, experienced, and, possibly, successful players. Don't be intimidated by big personalities, but do keep your wits about you.

Dedicated card rooms will be better organized than your average home game, with cashiers, dealers, floormen, and other employees all working to help make your time as enjoyable as possible. However, the nature of the game means that you will be expected to know the correct procedures with regard to betting and basic poker etiquette. Sure, plenty of folks out there will be only too willing to help out an inexperienced player who is unsure of themselves. But most will be more anxious to see the next hand and start betting again. Anyone who slows up the game will be made aware of it. Speed is of the essence in poker, and any player failing to keep pace with events will soon be at a disadvantage, quite apart from being considered a sucker by his opponents.

Still, everyone has to start somewhere and nobody can be expected to know everything straight away. To help you navigate this situation successfully, the key thing is to adopt a frame of mind geared to playing poker. That may sound obvious, but if you intend to play seriously, you have to think seriously. Since there is plenty to learn from observation at the table, perhaps you should approach playing in a card room in the same way as attending a college lecture. You'll be in the company of players more knowledgeable than yourself, but that doesn't mean you have nothing of value to contribute aside from your chips.

Adopt an attitude consistent with being a poker player who is learning and working toward something better. Set yourself realistic targets and discover from your experiences how best and how quickly you can reach them. The alternative is to be little more than a poker tourist, which is fine so long as you don't mind returning home after your poker vacation minus some of your spending money.

BELOW
Las Vegas—poker central—is the jewel in the Nevada Desert that lures world champions and amateur players alike.

ONLINE POKER STRATEGY

Most of what has been discussed already will apply to playing poker in online card rooms, at least when it comes to deploying a bit of tactical acumen relevant to the game you are playing. Wild and loose "play money" games exist next to no-limit games played for real money in Hold 'Em, Omaha and Seven Card Stud, to name just a few. With up to ten players sitting at a table, a tight and cautious approach is recommended until you feel comfortable with a game, even if you elect to play in a low-stakes contest.

Of course, as you cannot see the mannerisms and body language of your opponents, or hear any chat around the table, it can take some time to assess the prevailing mood. There is a textbox where players can enter brief messages but that cannot substitute for the immediacy of a live game. Also, only the scrolling textbox and visual representation on the screen indicate what is happening. The information comes thick and fast with a typical Hold 'Em hand taking just a minute or two, leaving you little time to monitor and absorb subtleties in play.

RIGHT
As you can see, there are a variety of popular games permanently in operation. Choose a game to suit your taste and skill. This picture highlights some Seven-Card Stud opportunities.

When entering an online poker room, you can select a table at which to play and simply watch the action. Be clinical. Try to evaluate the strength of the competition and the bankroll they have at their disposal. If you can see an opportunity for some low-risk fun, perhaps even a profit, settle down and take it. Bearing in mind that your position at the table is crucial, be selective when you choose your seat. Do you want to be acting behind or ahead of the player who is currently chip leader? If you sit to their left, you could quickly find yourself under pressure as they try using their chip lead to intimidate you. Of course, there's nothing to stop you from adopting the same strategy against a player low on chips to *your* left.

Also bear in mind you can switch from a fixed-limit game to a no-limit contest. Be prepared to change gear quickly because opponents will soon pressurize you with much larger bets. Be patient. They could be bluffing but you'll be more comfortable making a call when you possess a good hand.

RIGHT TOP
A starting hand in a no-limit game of Texas Hold 'Em. When switching from fixed-limit games, remember to adjust your style to accommodate more aggressive betting.

RIGHT
The showdown at a Texas Hold 'Em game and the Big Slick (A K) loses to J J. The anonymous winner, hidden behind a nickname, collects a pot of $4.55.

TOURNAMENT PLAY

Most guides to poker offer tips on tournament play ar
this is no exception. Anyone eager to discover an in-dep
approach to the subject is respectfully directed to books k
seriously good poker players such as Tom McEvoy, Doy
Brunson, and David Sklansky.

Doyle "Texas Dolly" Brunson, a former Worl
Champion, identified that no-limit Hold 'Em frequent
involved players waiting for a premium starting han
before luring the unwary into the pot. To combat this, h
found value in playing medium pairs and connectir
cards which, given a favorable flop, would often brea
these high-card hands. Of course, his opponents cottone
on to this strategy in the end but not until he ha
financially exploited it to the hilt. Sklansky, meanwhile,
a prolific writer on poker games and tournament pla
who explains a range of theories in such detail tha
virtually every poker book I've ever read refers to hin
That must be recommendation enough.

However, as this book is intended for the beginner, it
assumed that you won't be coughing up the $10,000 entr
fee for the World Series of Poker just yet. Nevertheles
despite the inherent differences between low-stakes cas
games and tournament poker, it cannot hurt to absorb
few basic lessons that might be useful in your home gam
Adjusting your style of play and changing gear throughor
a tournament are valuable skills in such a competitiv
arena. It stands to reason that you must be observar
picking up clues from the sources of information availabl
to you at the table. As the prospect of reaching the fina
table beckons, and with it a share of the prize pool, player
may tighten up their play to protect their chip positior
This can be used to your advantage by playing a littl
more loosely, since players may be reluctant to bet wit
anything but premium cards. But don't play too fast to
early because there are no prizes for being chip leade
after a couple of hours when the tournament lasts for
week. It might only take one bad beat to send you packing

Compare this with your home game where thos
players eager for betting action may be buying-in for mor
chips before they've finished their first beer. Equally, if th
session is drawing to a close and you are well up on th
night, why commit your chips to lost causes in a round c
wild-card variations that offer no value? Play it tightly an
go home a winner instead. In a tournament, when you'r
ahead, you can afford to ease off the gas and let the othe
players knock each other out. The same basic theor
applies to cash games.

WATCH THE STACKS

In tournaments, the scale of the blinds rises continually, guaranteeing that players must make a move or risk being blinded away. Observing their chip stacks can give you a clue regarding the value of hand your opponents might play. The fewer chips they have, the more likely they are to take a risk. The experts also recommend that you take note of the average size of the stacks around the table. This helps you to determine whether you are ahead or behind in the game and dictates your strategy accordingly. If you're falling behind, you have to get busy and that means playing the cards you're dealt. Even if they don't promise nirvana, you can still play them. And that's because suggesting you have good cards can be enough to win a pot. Should you ever play in a tournament, the chances are you'll face this situation. At that point, making a potentially crippling bet to suggest you have a premium hand may be the only chance you have of staying in the game.

Bluffing, as indicated elsewhere, is a potent weapon in no-limit and pot-limit tournaments when you are in an advantageous chip position. Pressurizing someone who cannot afford to lose might be ruthless, but nobody said winning was easy. Similarly, when you detect a player is under pressure in a low-stakes game, gauge how much he wants to risk going "down to the cloth." If he really doesn't want to risk losing all his money right there and then, a bluff might well be successful. He'll be wondering why you should make a risky bet when you've already won enough to treat everybody to a night on the town.

Another ruthless aspect of tournament play involves putting an opponent all-in when they have relatively few chips remaining. For example, if a player bets half his $2,000 stack and you are sitting on $25,000 with the intention of calling, why not raise him the additional $1,000? You wouldn't be calling if you had no chance of winning the hand and, logically, it makes sense to try knocking out your opponent at the same time.

Even in fixed-limit poker, a successful session could see you with sufficient chips to raise any bet from a short-stacked player without risk of a seriously damaging loss. Consequently, if players want to win back chips from you, they will normally try to do so only when they are holding very good hands; they cannot afford to do otherwise.

Timing in poker is extremely important and never more so than when playing at the highest level. Exploiting your position in the betting round is crucial as this will often dictate whether or not you risk a huge stack of chips,

BELOW
This Hold 'Em flop example presents a chance to pressurize an opponent into raising despite being low on chips.

even if you do not have a great hand. Should players t your right be in a situation where they are much lower o chips than you, you have a chance to steal the blinds or rais any bet already made, which could leave their stack serious depleted if they call. In that situation, the quality of your han is not as important to your opponents as what will happen they call and lose. Again it demonstrates the power that is your disposal to bluff or semi-bluff when playing no-lim poker and finding yourself with a big chip lead.

Yet the same proposition can be replicate in your home game. Let's assume you and you buddies are playing $1–$2 limit Hold 'Em wit a maximum of three raises per betting round You all started with $50 but now the guy to you right is down to his last $15 and you have $9. He bets a dollar before the flop and you rais another $1. Someone else raises again befor the action reaches our victim. You can tell h wants to raise. He probably has a good hand— a high pair, As maybe, or A K suited—and h needs to reduce the field to improve the odds o his winning. But a call costs $2 and a final rais in this round is going to cost him $3. He raise and now has just $11 left, but the pot is alread temptingly big and he hasn't seen the flop ye You call.

XPLOITING WEAKNESS

e knows you can match his bets without
amaging your stack and is also aware that you
ould possess any two cards at all. The flop comes
hearts, 8 spades, 2 diamonds. If he has a pair of
s, he'd probably like to bet and if he thinks of a
eckraise, he knows that you might just raise him
ack again. You can pressurize him with the chips
your disposal, leaving him unable to tell whether
e flop has hit your hand or not.

So he bets another $1 and you raise again.
veryone else folds, so he calls. That's another $2 he's put in
e pot and, with just $9 left, the betting is about to go up.
he turn card is 8 clubs. Now you really want him to have a
air of As, Ks, or something similar. The pair of 8s on the
oard allied to your willingness to match any bet he makes
as got to make him anxious. For all the bravado and macho
osturing you may be indulging in with your mighty stack,
ou just might be playing 9 8 suited, 8 7 suited, or even 8
nything offsuit, if you're feeling reckless. The point is, he
nows you can afford it. He bets $2—perhaps he has two pair,
hich could well be enough—and you re-raise again.

With just $7 left, a call of $2 required to see the river card,
nd absolutely no idea whether he is winning or not, by now
e is pretty much committed to the pot. But that $7
presents a comfortable ride home in a taxi. Can he risk it?

There's no need to take the hand to its conclusion and,
any case, even if you won you'd hardly send your pal
way without the fare home. But the point is there was an
pportunity to exploit a player's weakness and you didn't
eed a decent hand with which to do it. In tournament
lay, the only difference is that the low-stacked player
sks waving goodbye to their chance at the main prize.
f they stand to finish 21st when the prize pool extends
the top twenty, they are
ame's the same and the
oves are the same, it's only
he context that is different.

ABOVE
A player with a low
stack may be
intimidated even
when holding a pair
of Aces.

RIGHT
In the face of
aggressive betting,
your opponent may
put you on 9 8 or
8 7 suited.

BLUFFING

The situation used as an example at the end of the previous section leads us neatly into a few ideas on bluffing. It illustrates that, with the chip count in your favor and the advantage of betting subsequent to the player under most pressure, the actual value of your hand receded in importance. Your opponent knew you could be bluffing with a trash hand but what could they do about it? The important point is that it was a good moment to contemplate a bluff, assuming that you didn't have the cards to beat them anyway. But before we consider the timing of the bluff, why is it such a crucial part of the game?

In short, the bluff is the one element of poker that helps separate winning from losing. Theorists will confirm that if several risk-averse players of equal knowledge and ability play an almost infinite number of hands over many years, eventually they will be back where they started. Each will get lucky, hitting good hands that lose and poor hands that win until all probabilities are exhausted and their chip stacks are as they were at the outset. Everyone breaks even.

A TACTICAL WEAPON

If you want to win, you have to take risks and that's where bluffing comes into play. Suggesting to an opponent that your hand is strong with a big bet is the tactical weapon required to convert breaking even into making a handsome profit. By creating doubt in your adversary's mind, you remind them of the risks inherent in any gambling proposition and you test their resolve. If they crack, you win the pot. Of course, bluffing with a weak hand until all your opponents fold is the classic conceptual notion. But how can you present yourself with an opportunity to really make it happen?

One common situation is related to your position in the betting round. Again, the importance of position cannot be overstated when it comes to your strategies at the table. Suppose you are on the dealer button in a game of Hold 'Em, the flop is assorted, unpaired medium or low cards—9 hearts, 8 clubs, 2 diamonds, for example—and everyone has checked to you. If they've checked because they have moderate hands, then everyone almost expects you to bet on account of the apparent weakness, irrespective of the cards you hold. If your hand is moderate, too, at worst you'll weed out the weak hands and discover if someone out there is slow playing something better.

OPPOSITE
To get to grips with the concept of bluffing, imagine you're the player in this illustration of Hold 'Em and the flop comes 9 8 2.

PLAYER'S HAND

BOARD CARDS

OPPONENT'S HAND

A TIME TO BLUFF

Maybe you'll be checkraised, but that needn't cost you much if your bet equates to the marketing budget rather than the whole company. You can fold and lose your money without experiencing too many qualms. Does that suggest the bluff didn't work? For that hand, maybe, but remember, you've just advertised that you are prepared to back a hand that may not immediately look like a winner. That can come in useful.

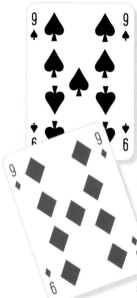

Suppose, in this example, that you are called by a couple of players and then the turn card, 8 spades, pairs the board. Your opponents check again and you bet. There is no flush possibility, but a straight draw is still on for anyone holding Q J, J 10, J 7, 7 6, or 6. Maybe one player has two pair, but which two pair? Even a full house is possibly being slow played? The point here is, all three of you could be thinking the same thing. And if nobody has hit the nut hand yet, who is going to bet like they have?

At this stage, it is worth highlighting the obvious: most bluffs should be considered when facing very few opponents. Ideally, you want a heads-up situation against just one opponent, especially in a game like Hold 'Em or Stud where the face-up cards can cause havoc with a player's imagination. As the hand develops and betting becomes more intense, is usually safe to assume a player has a good hand if they are still in the game. But bluffing challenges this assumption and tests a player's willingness to take a risk.

GATHERING INFORMATION

Bluffing can help you to gather information about your opponents. Continuing with our example, let's say you actually hold 5 hearts, 4 spades—a dreadful hand in this situation, with no draw and the pair of 8s common to all. Any card higher than a 5 is beating you, let alone another pair. But you bet again anyway. One opponent folds and the other calls.

The river card is 9 spades, giving two pair on the board. Your opponent checks and you are sure that they have at least one card bigger than your 5. The only way you can win the pot is to bluff. Even if they have an 8 in their hand giving them a full house, they would be wary of you having the 9 for bigger one. If they have the 9 already, then they're luring you into a bet and inducing a bluff. You calculate that you are prepared to risk a few more chips in this hand, but that you expect to be called. What do you do? Well, let's say that you bluff, risking just enough chips to ask a polite question without damaging your longer term prospects in the game.

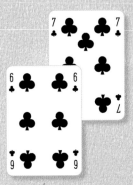

Betting after a flop of
9 8 2 may suggest you
are holding any of
these five examples.

WILLINGNESS TO DECEIVE

Your opponent calls and reveals A clubs, 8 diamonds, giving them a full house to your two pair with a 5 kicker. The bluff was exposed and your willingness to deceive—to lie, in effect—has been demonstrated to all. Embarrassing, perhaps, but morality in poker is restricted to playing by the rules of the game, not misrepresenting the strength of your cards. So now that everyone knows you'll take on a risky proposition, how can they judge the strength of your hand the next time you make any kind of bet? Perhaps next time you have a pair of As and be in a poor position as the first to act. A big bet then will have everyone thinking that you either have a fantastic hand or that you are making a sharp move with moderate cards. They may even believe that you are bluffing outrageously, but they are going to have to pay to find out and that is the key to the whole concept.

By showing your willingness to bluff, you are setting up the possibility that, when you do have the best hand, others will be unable to read it as such until it's too late. And when you win, you want to win the maximum available. Advertising your willingness to deceive is the best way to encourage opponents to bet against you when you do have the goods. Referring to the game given as an example, maybe next time a similar hand develops you'll be sitting with a pair in the hole, hit your full house, and nobody will suspect it until they get wiped out.

Though you may lose a pot with a bluff, you can generate something else very important to your prospects and that respect. It is said that if you are never caught bluffing, you probably aren't bluffing enough and are playing far too tightly. As a result, you may not be winning as much as you could, and that's a waste of talent if you're a decent player. Conversely, if you feel that your bluffs are always called, then you must be trying it too often and need to re-examine your style. Perhaps you are not reading the play very well or maybe you need to overcome that tendency to stay in the pot even when you are sure you are losing, "just in case."

In low-stakes poker, trying to bluff someone who insists on calling all the way to the showdown is pointless. Similarly, a poor player who cannot see what hand you are implying with a bet is not worth bluffing either, since they are not familiar

ABOVE
Your opponent's 8 diamonds matches the board to give a full house. That easily beats your two pair of 9s and 8s with a 5 kicker.

nough with the game to understand the trouble they could be acing. In such situations, David Sklansky's idea of the semi-bluff represents a better policy. As such, you will have a hand hat you think is losing, hence the bluff, but it's not so desperate hat you cannot hit cards that will make it a winner. Playing t a higher level, the semi-bluff with reasonable cards in our hand, rather than the naked bluff when you hold othing, is a viable tactic.

That briefly covers some of the theoretical factors of luffing, but reading your opponents, understanding their ame, and calculating when a bluff may work best also equires observation. The cards may help dictate the moment o practice a little deception, but playing poker is all about laying people. So, in the next chapter, we'll take a look at ow body language and a little psychology can help.

BELOW
Observing your opponents' mannerisms during a game can provide you with many clues.

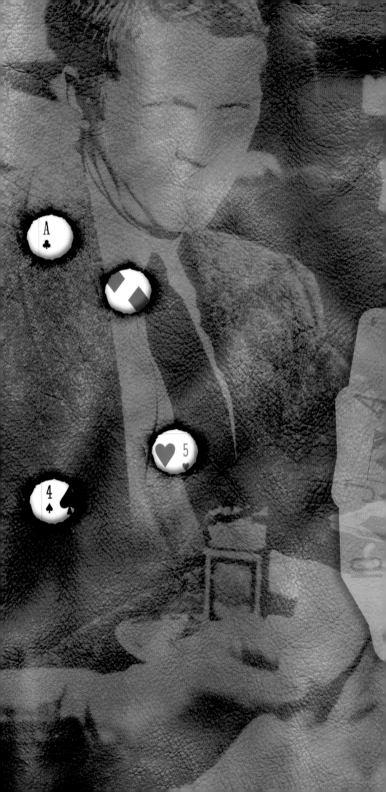

BODY LANGUAGE

The previous chapter explained some of the factors that a budding poker player needs to consider when sitting in at a game. Choosing what game to play and what strategies to adopt have so far entered into consideration. But, as mentioned earlier, people play poker because of its competitive nature.

This fact brings with it all kinds of challenges, since each poker player is a unique individual in his or her own right. Much of what has been covered so far concentrates on the technical and mechanical aspects of play. Yet we all know that it is the human element, the desire to compete and to win, that elevates poker above the mundane. Wit, imagination, intuition, blind faith—all have their place within the human psyche and are not excused duty at the poker table. On the face of it, determining information from the actions and mannerisms of opponents might seem too tricky when so much else is happening during a poker game. You cannot read their minds, now, can you? Probably not, but a million years of social interaction has endowed human beings with a wide range of subconscious gestures and mannerisms. These may have been subordinated to the development of speech, but the signals we communicate without realizing are often very revealing. The ability to spot these gestures and comprehend their meaning will enhance your prospects at the poker table, and an awareness of their presence might help you gain control over some of your own involuntary movements.

..aving a poker face ..handy but I don't ..hink I can squint ..ke this all night.

LEFT
Involuntary facial expressions can say a lot about the cards you hold and that may restrict your winnings.

LOOKING FOR CLUES

In considering the impact that body language can have on your poker game, you need to take into account what you can hear from the inevitable chat around the table and, to start with, what you can see. What visible clues are evident to help you judge a player's mood, their hand, and their prospects? Do their actions reveal useful information that you can exploit to your advantage?

To give yourself a chance of finding out, the first thing you must do is watch the other players at the table. It may be obvious, but the novice player is all too often coming to grips with the rules and betting structures of a game and will not be able to focus on what they regard as peripheral factors. Playing experience will help the beginner become more skilled in calculating betting decisions and tactics at speed. Only then will the benefits of studying other players become apparent, because they have a little more time available to acquire additional information. But how does all this help?

First, assuming that you would rather win at poker more often than you lose, interpreting the various signals and subliminal messages given off by a player's gestures might just make a difference. Of equal importance, watching how your opponents react in different situations can

He's looking mighty nervous. It could be time for a big bet.

elp you focus on your own mannerisms. If you detect a "tell"
 one of your opponents, in other words, if they telegraph the
al strength of their hand with a subconscious gesture, it may
ert you to a similar tendency you possess when in the same
tuation. Watching others helps you become self-aware and
ore self-critical, in a poker sense, and will help you to control
ur own body language.

So what exactly are you looking for when trying to detect
 this additional information? The simplest way to approach
is question is to consider the basic elements inherent in
aying poker: handling cards, handling chips, and focusing on
e game. While there cannot be any firm assurances that the
oservations you make will be accurate, once you have picked
o a way of reading an opponent's moves, you have the
ance to adjust your strategy accordingly. That could win you
ore chips or, equally important, save you a few bad losses.

As for yourself, the ideal posture to adopt is one that
ggests you are unworried, in control, and exuding a patient
nse of calm amid the poker storm. Treat your fortunate wins
d bad beats in exactly the same fashion and you may
ell be in the envious position of never giving away the
rength of your hand or your betting intentions.

BELOW
By observing an opponent you may detect mannerisms that indicate the strength of his hand.

He's looking mighty nervous. He must be bluffing again.

CARDS IN THE HAND

Let's start with a simple game of Draw Poker featuring fiv
players at the table. If it helps, picture our buddies from earli
in the book, Wild Bill, Doc, Annie, Calamity, and Jesse. Wh
can be determined from the way players handle their cards
a game like this?

The nature of the game means that players will physical
hold their cards in their hand while considering whether
bet and how many cards to draw. Generally, when th
cards are initially dealt, each player should wait until th
deal is complete before checking their hand. But son
players cannot wait that long. If they are s
impatient to see what fate has dealt them, wh
does this say about their style of play? Th
chances are they are going to make hasty decisio
in a bid to generate some action. If so, a patie
approach could well pay off as you wait to capitali
on their impetuosity.

Then there is the player who is so keen to obscure the
cards from opponents that they clutch them tightly to the
chest the whole time, peering at them as if they might chan
at any moment. This doesn't seem like the action of a relaxe
player but suggests someone who is suspicious of everythin
In a sense, that may be wise with everyone else out to w
chips. But the paranoia can stretch a bit too far if they have
wait for the nuts before venturing a bet. If they think the
opponents are really after them, they are going to be very wa
of falling into a trap. That makes it easier to bluff them out
a pot from time to time, particularly with a re-raise, since th
will be inclined to believe that such a move must indicate a bett
hand. Playing too tightly could be ruining their game.

Then there's the player who fans his cards out casual
looking at them with disdain and rearranging them in his han
to try to make them represent a hand worth playin
Maybe they really do have a load of trash but it could
a little act they are implementing to mislea
opponents. Should they fold, then you might fe
you've read them right. But if you bet, they call an
when the draw comes, they take just the one car
you could be up against a big two pair with chanc
of a full house, or a nut flush draw. Either way, th
dismissive air could have lulled you into making a ris
bet, so be careful.

Moving on to games like Texas Hold 'Em, Omaha an
Stud, holding your hole cards in your hand is not exactly co
Players should ensure their cards are clearly visible to the
opponents at all times to indicate their continued participatic
in a hand. So a glance at your hole cards, perhaps by gent
turning up the corners, to determine what you hold.

Of course, some hands are easier to remember than others. Taking Hold 'Em, for example, with just two cards to examine before making a bet it shouldn't be difficult to remember what you have after the flop materializes. A pair of black As, Ks, or Qs in the hole is going to burn itself into your consciousness without too much trouble. And when you hit trips on the flop, the fact that you bet quickly without looking at your hole cards is likely to transmit a warning to your opponents. Then again, you could very well be bluffing.

ABOVE
Exuding an air of cool, calm control is an asset at the poker table.

But what if you have A 5 offsuit and the flop comes up K, 2, 3 diamonds? You thought the Ace was worth playing and now all you can recall is that it was red, not black. Have you got the draw to the nut flush with the A diamonds, or was it the A hearts? You're going to have to check and everyone will recognize your dilemma. Some of them may have the same problem but, in an easygoing game, that is par for the course. In fact, it becomes a bit of a joke among the players themselves.

The point is valid, though. You've checked the A and it's a heart, not a diamond. What now? OK, the only other player who knows you do not have the A diamonds would be the player lucky enough to see it amid their own hole cards. You might be able to bet to represent the flush, or the flush draw anyway, but nobody has you down for a pair of Ks in the hole, that's for sure. Memory is important in poker and that doesn't just extend to keeping track of folded-up cards during a game of Stud.

In general, if a player looks frequently at their hole cards, then the likely reasons for this are threefold. First, he could be a poor player who cannot calculate how good his hand is, let alone what he might be up against. Second, he may be impatient to get on with the action suggesting he is itching to bet with a big hand. And third, perhaps the liquid refreshment or the lateness of the hour has simply interfered with his powers of recall.

> **REMEMBERING YOUR HOLE CARDS**
> ◆
> It may seem obvious, but if you are trying to conceal as much as possible from your opponents, it makes sense to memorise your hole cards. Omaha, with four cards to consider, is more testing than Hold 'Em, but it has to be an advantage not to be seen checking for flush draws or, perhaps, a low kicker that suddenly pairs the board for you.

RIGHT
Remembering your hole cards is a good idea, but you won't always be dealt a hand as easy to recall as this example.

CARDS IN HAND 1

CARDS IN HAND 2

Hold 'Em hands such as these high pairs of the same color suit are easy to remember.

CARDS IN HAND 3

HOLE CARDS

When the flop reveals three diamonds, can you remember whether your red A was a diamond or a heart?

FLOP CARDS

CHIPS ON THE TABLE

After considering how different players tend to handle their cards, what about the way they handle their chips? Are your regular opponents inclined to fiddle with a few chips in their hand all through the game? Do they stack them up neatly, and draw them in close to the body? Or do they leave them scattered randomly on the table in front of them?

Anyone who cannot resist the tactile joys of holding a chip or two in their hand during a game may come across as a slightly anxious individual. Perhaps even this nervous behavior is a manifestation of the player's urgent need to be close to the action, ready to bet as soon as the chance arises.

At any stage of a game, as soon as you see a player fondly examining their chips and maybe separating a few from the rest of their stack, it's a fair assumption that they are thinking about a bet. Or, of course, that could be exactly what they want you to think. It may be that they are bluffing with a heavy hint that you shouldn't bet, since they may not have a hand good enough with which to call if you do. Here, your knowledge of the player and your understanding of their moves will help you to extract some meaning from their actions. The benefits of experience and observation are emphasized once again.

BELOW LEFT
Noting how players stack their chips can be helpful. Neat orderly stacks suggest a tidy and thoughtful approach.

STAKING THE CHIPS
◆

While it may not offer too many clues on the quality of any particular hand, how players place their chips in the pot may give an indication of their general demeanor. The recommended practice is to place the chips that you bet in a neat stack in front of you. That way everyone has a quick visual clue as to the scale of the betting and how much they need to bet should they be required to call, for instance. A slow and deliberate motion with the chips would appear to indicate that a player wants their hand to be taken seriously. At the other extreme, some players insist on splashing the pot with their chips, if only to make a statement that they are rebellious enough not to adhere to protocol. And that could mean some pretty wild betting decisions are their stock in trade.

CHIP STACKS

How do you like to stack your chips when playing? Do you keep them in neat piles, one for each denomination? Or do you prefer to mix and match them, paying little attention to them until you have to make a bet? Whichever example applies to you, the possibility exists that you could be giving away a clue to your play. Neat, orderly stacks can suggest a player who likes to play a controlled and methodical game. If that is the case, they may not take too many risks. The reverse can be true of the untidy player. Maybe their style is as loose and disheveled as their chips.

If you've watched poker on television or witnessed a few professional tournaments in the flesh, you will probably have noticed that many players are inclined to put a chip or a lucky charm on their hole cards. This has a practical application in that it indicates that the hand is in play and prevents it from being mucked inadvertently. But what if a player only exhibits this tendency occasionally? Surely that indicates something significant?

For my money, such behavior would suggest that the hand on this occasion is of the utmost importance to the player. Under no circumstances is this one to be mixed up with the discards. So the advice is to keep a very watchful eye on his betting moves from here on in since he evidently wants to support these cards if he possibly can.

Beware the player who looks at their cards and immediately makes what they consider an imperceptible glance at their chips. Again, this player is already calculating what they can afford to bet or how much they should stake to maximize chances of winning. If you know them to be a player that calls almost every bet, irrespective of their cards, perhaps you shouldn't be alarmed. But someone you suspect is a competent player with a few moves up their sleeve might just have given you an insight into their plans.

Obviously, monitoring how a player manages their chips is not a foolproof way of predicting their betting moves every time. But if you spot something quirky or unusual about their play and see it repeated under similar circumstances, maybe you can read their moves in advance. It all helps.

CHIP SELECTION

Chips come in various denominations and, as the game proceeds, these will be distributed around the table. At some stage a player may have a sizeable quantity of either small or large denominations at their disposal. If they bet using two large value chips rather than a handful of smaller ones, do you think they are expecting them back very quickly? Most of us hate to break into a big note when we have small change available, and perhaps this player is the same. On the other hand, if a bet is made with a big stack of lower denomination chips, perhaps the player is happy to risk losing them if only to clear some space in front of them. It's a thought.

ARE YOU LOOKING AT ME?

Every now and again, a player is going to give you the eye and stare at you to generate some kind of reaction. Maybe you've just put in a big raise and they want to see if you flinch, indicating that you're bluffing. On the other hand, they may have put in the big bet and are daring you to call. Either way, if you have the best hand, it isn't going to make any difference. The act is one of implied threat and is designed to ward you away from a confrontation, but it cannot affect the cards. If it does bother you, wear a hat and sunglasses and keep your head well down.

PAUSE FOR THOUGHT

Poker is a quick game in which players expect the action to circulate around the table without undue delay. On the basis that every losing hand brings them nearer their next winner, poker players want to see cards and start betting. But for the beginner, pausing to work out the implications of a hand is a necessary part of the learning process. Of course, if it takes you too long to figure out your chances, you probably have no chance at all and everyone will spot it. But when an experienced player takes their time, it usually means that they are "showboating" by putting on a little act. Rest assured that, unless the World Series of Poker title depends on it, they probably have a great hand that they want to disguise as something vastly inferior.

FOCUSING ON THE GAME

So, we've had a look at what players mig do when handling their cards and the chips, and explored some of the meaning that may be hidden behind vario gestures. If some of their person characteristics are reflected in the mannerisms at the card table, you hav a chance to gain a psychologic advantage.

The timid and suspicious play who jealously protects his cards an chips may well be susceptible to sizeable bluffing bet. If they're tha tense, how can they call withou possessing the absolute nuts? On th other hand, a loose player that yo know likes to contest every pot ripe for a little strategic plotting Since you expect them to call on regular basis, why not play a fe wildly speculative hands to th showdown, as cheaply as possible course, and let them take a few pots fro you. By the time you hit a certain winne they may well be expecting you to be o some crazy flush or straight draw agai and match you bet for bet. Make sure yo put enough in the pot to reap the benefi of their misjudgment.

Apart from the physical signs o excitement or disappointment, such as a upright posture, trembling hands, or eve some heavy perspiration, be aware of othe indicators of tension on display.

When a player is having trouble depositin chips in the pot because of the shakes, th chances are they are struck with anxiety at bein close to a victory. Closing in on one's pre gets the adrenaline pumping, however, an keeping that discreetly obscured from the othe players is difficult.

Another sign of anxiety generated by the sigh of a good hand is exhibited when a player acts ou of turn. Folding out of turn is poor play and offer free additional information to players who may b betting before you. Instead of making a small bet they may opt for a bigger one now that the field ha been reduced ahead of schedule.

DON'T BE DISTRACTED

❖

Finding yourself distracted during the game is very easy, though not recommended. Depending on where you are playing, there could be music, television, food, flashing lights and plenty of chat in the room. But let's suppose you hit a good hand and you want to fool everyone into thinking the opposite. By acting as though you are more interested in the game on television than the cards, you are demanding a very good performance from yourself. The chances of it succeeding are dependent on the experience of your opponents. Generally, such fakery is easily spotted, especially if it seems out of character.

Then there is the player who advertises their enthusiasm for his hand by announcing a bet before it is his turn to act. In this instance, they are likely to have cost themselves a few extra chips because such urgency can only mean that they are equipped to go the distance. If you exhibit such impatience, it will irritate your opponents and cost you money. Good opportunities can take a while to appear, so why waste one through inattention to detail?

Players who call quickly, especially in earlier and cheaper betting rounds, may be communicating a pessimistic view of their chances without realizing it. Though they are acting in turn, they haven't taken long to make a decision, suggesting they still need help before going for glory. In the later stages of a game when a heads-up situation might develop, so much information is available to the players that a quick call, or even a raise, usually means the bet is a confident one. That's good if you make the raise but extremely threatening if you're the player on the receiving end.

I won't be distracted. I'm staying with this pot until the bitter end.

VERBAL WARNINGS

The section on poker etiquette toward the end of the next chapter discusses the differing attitudes to talking during a hand. In the United States, it is accepted as almost integral to the game to have players trying to rattle each other with a few misleading, or even derogatory, comments. The intimacy of a home game among friends might be considered a bit too frosty without them.

Elsewhere, discussion about hands, both during play and at their conclusion, is considered bad manners. Internationally, tournaments adhere to strict rules about players alerting others to the cards they possess, whether they are trying to intimidate and mislead opponents or not. Stiff penalties can be incurred for breaking the code of conduct.

Yet a poker game is a magnet for willful individuals not shy of expressing themselves one way or another. As a result, plenty of audible signals will be given off as players tire, become despondent, or try to shake others off their scent. I've lost count of the times when, toward the end of a sociable poker session with ready access to a few beers, I've uttered an expletive at being dealt yet another 7 2 offsuit in a game of Hold 'Em. It rather gives the game away, to be honest, and it also means that a barefaced bluff is then out of the question.

BELOW
Avoid goading opponents by discussing your hand or theirs. In tournaments, you may be punished with a stiff penalty.

milarly, clues come in the form of the player who slumps
ack in his chair with a huge sigh and a resigned thud. They
re either an excellent actor or they know they are about to
se another hand. That's enough to upset anyone, but the
gh is hardly subtle. As bluffs go, it doesn't usually work too
ell either, since only truly excellent actors can pull that
f. When you laugh at the way Dame Fortune treads on
our toes once again, secure in the knowledge you're
bout to fold, you have no intention of hiding anything.
ut when you've just hit a full house on the flop and
ou want to suggest disappointment, too much
elodrama will send the audience home.

Another audible clue to the state of play in a game comes
hen a player, seemingly distracted, asks whether it is their
rn to bet. If you are puzzled that such a typically attentive
layer seems to have lost the plot, it might be because they
now exactly whose bet it is. Be very careful. On the other
and, if the player who always asks whose bet it is when the
ction reaches them should utter the question yet
gain, it simply proves they ought to take up
mething less demanding
an a game of poker.

A lynching for chatting at the poker table? No wonder they call it the Wild West!

WHERE TO PLAY

B y now you should have a fair idea of what poker is, how to play, and what you need to consider before participating in a game. If you fancy hosting a poker session, you also have a guide to the basic equipment you'll need for a successful and enjoyable time. But apart from your own home, where else can you play?

Throughout the book, references have been made to home games, card rooms, casinos, and online poker sites. These constitute the majority of places to play. The intention of this section is to highlight some of the features of each potential venue to make you feel a little more comfortable when confronted with a new environment.

If you wish, it is even possible to play poker via your cellphone. Phil Hellmuth Jr., the self-styled poker brat and undoubtedly one of the best players in the world, has lent his name to a Texas Hold 'Em service offered for subscription in May 2004. Online poker, which has developed incredibly over the past five years, continues to grow in popularity, and it constitutes another chance for you to become involved in poker without leaving home. And as home games are the mainstay of poker, that is where we shall start.

BELOW
Some clubs and casinos will offer a higher class of service than others.

I'm sorry sir, but the game is over. Come back same time next week.

HOME GAMES

Various factors involved in playing in a private game at home have already been mentioned in the chapters on Game Strategies and Body Language. Also, in terms of poker etiquette, the section toward the end of this chapter offers tips on how to conduct yourself in a manner that will earn respect. At any table, but particularly when playing among friends and acquaintances in a regular game, you surely want to be respected enough to warrant an invitation to play again. But that doesn't mean you shouldn't have a bit of fun if the social mix around the table is right.

Each poker school will have its cast of characters and personalities giving the session a dynamic of its own. You can expect one player to be the driving force behind everything, from organizing the game to constantly suggesting a new variation to play. They may well be an accountant of some description, too, so you can expect him to play banker with the

ABOVE
There are two ways to earn respect at the table. Good play is one, and exhibiting a courteous regard for your opponents and the rules is another.

hips and keep a weather eye out for betting discrepancies. Usually there's a player to whom everyone defers when it comes to contentious situations. Calm and studious, their knowledge commands respect even if their play is far from the most profitable. Also among the cast will be the player who wants to chat all night, catching up with the news and focusing on anything else but poker. Obviously, they never knows when it's their turn to bet since they are too preoccupied with listening to a discussion on last night's ball game. Amiable but frustrating, it always hurts when they beat you, although they tend to end up a loser most of the time.

Similarly there is always one player who obligingly participates in every hand until, suddenly, they realize that they haven't won a pot all night and had better start playing. When they do, they invariably hit the second-best hand and start muttering about the injustice of the game and how someone should take pity on them for their losses. By way of contrast, there is likely to be a big stack of chips building up in front of the player whose judgment, you'd guess, ought to be severely impaired by the influence of their other love—whiskey.

Music is a favored accompaniment to home games and this is something else that can distract the average player. It also generates conversations on subjects other than sports and poker, handy if you want to invite a poker-playing rock fan, but not so good if each hand takes longer to play than a Ted Nugent guitar solo.

Find these characters in your game and you can expect some chaotic, frustrating, and sometimes hilarious poker, which isn't always about scooping pots and winning all the money.

BELOW
Some background music can help a home game go with a swing. Just make sure nobody comes armed with a guitar.

Hey cowboy, don't suppose you know "Ace of Spades" by Motorhead, do you?

179

CASINOS AND CARD ROOMS

A typical home game may be light-hearted, chaotic and, if the beers are flowing freely, quite disorganized by the end of the session. The card room experience in a casino will be none of these things, even if, on your first visit, the number of people milling around give that impression.

Casinos operate to make money and they are generally very good at it. As such, most of the gambling opportunities they offer are geared to maintaining that situation. Yes, it is possible to win big at Keno, Blackjack, Roulette, Craps, and even on the slot machines. But the conditions under which these games operate are such that the casino has a guaranteed profit margin. For instance, if you bet $1 on each number available on a roulette wheel, it would cost you $38 for numbers 1 to 36 plus the zero and double-zero. Yet, whichever of these comes up, you will only be paid $36 (odds of 35 to 1) for your trouble. The casino takes $2 just for spinning the wheel. Multiply that concept to accommodate the vast numbers of people gambling for fun and you will understand how casinos stay in business.

This brings us to the first important difference in casino play compared to that at home, namely, "the rake." This is a nominal amount deducted from each pot by the house to cover expenses. It's possible that a regular poker school may operate an agreed policy of skimming a little from the pot now and then to

ABOVE
Casino games like roulette pitch you against the house. In poker, you oppose the other players.

meet the costs of staging the entertainment. But in the casino, it is a fact of life that someone has to pay for the dealer, cashier, table, chairs, and chips. The chips at stake in the poker game itself are distributed between the players at the table since, unlike in Blackjack, they oppose each other, not the casino itself. The rake represents a fee for the facilities and it's also customary to tip the dealer when you win a pot. So even a winning session does not come without some expense.

Of course, with food and drink constantly on offer for the duration of your visit, casinos do have other ways of extracting money from your pockets, but at least they'll take it with a smile. Surely that's better than sitting at your local burger joint where poker is off the menu?

More seriously, the speed of play at casino tables and the competitive nature of the players can make for some daunting, if exciting, entertainment. Once you've chosen a game to play and decided on the stake level at which you wish to compete, be prepared to approach your game with a little caution. Watch your opponents and learn as much as you can before you start letting loose with those naked bluffs that always work against your buddies at home.

Also, be objective enough to imagine what constitutes success for you. It may be that you are happy to make $200 stretch to five or six hours before having to retire from the game. If you are on vacation and playing poker is how you like to relax, whether you win or lose, then this may be a realistic approach. And if you leave the table having tripled your money during a streak of poker fortune that defies probability, so much the better. But for a beginner, this is unlikely.

One other point to make about the casino experience is that the environment is geared toward cutting you off from the outside world. Time and the seasons mean nothing in these air-conditioned cocoons decorated with mirrors and artificial lighting. Like factories designed to shake the cash from your pockets, these high-class gambling dens can wear you down if you don't take care of yourself. That means regulating your time at the table and taking a break now and again for refreshment.

The level of concentration required to play well is difficult to sustain for long and you may be permitted to leave a game for a set time without losing your seat at the table entirely. Have a drink or a meal and return when you feel ready. If you really are exhausted, remember the casino is probably open 24 hours a day and a game will always be happening somewhere tomorrow.

CHOOSING A GAME

◆

This is the first crucial decision that faces a player who is new to the casino experience. Even if you have built up some knowledge of a particular variation, the speed of the play will come as a shock. Unless you are confident about the rules and what to do when it's your turn to act, you may start to feel a little lonely. Yes, the dealer and other players may help out a little, but they are certainly not obliged to do so. Any mistakes you make, especially in the general conduct of your play, will be punished as the more predatory players take advantage of your inexperience.

So stick to a game with which you are totally comfortable.

STAKE LEVELS

◆

Having decided on the game you wish to play and come to terms with the new environment, the next important consideration is your bankroll. How much will it cost you to enter a game? Since the stake levels will vary, the best advice is to opt for a game in which you can, with conservative play, enjoy a lengthy session. That is, after all, why you are in a casino. But the need to regard your chips at the table separately from your disposable cash is vital to playing without too much restraint. So calculate an amount that you feel you can comfortably afford to lose, and choose your game. If a $3–$6 fixed-limit game proves too dull, you can always take a break and consider moving up to a table where the stakes are higher.

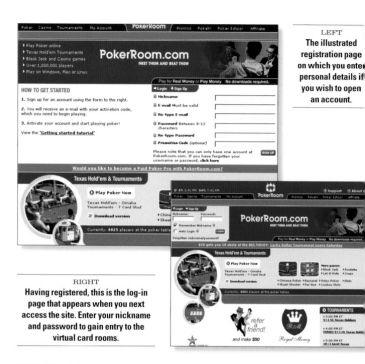

ONLINE POKER

There's no denying that the development of the internet has led to a massive increase in opportunities for people to find entertainment. From the technical to the lurid, there are websites to satisfy almost every aspect of human curiosity. And that means there is plenty of information about poker.

The burgeoning interest in the game can be squarely placed on the shoulders of rapid developments in the media. As soon as poker tournaments started being televised, the game's legendary players became more widely known. Autobiographical accounts of their exploits at the poker table and a plethora of poker guidebooks helped generate even more publicity for the game. Now we have the internet, which not only provides access to virtually everything there is to know about poker, but also acts as a barometer of poker's global popularity.

Armed with a low-grade Personal Computer (PC), a 56K modem and access to a telephone line, it is possible to engage in real poker games with players from all over the world. You can play for real money, too, as long as you have a valid credit card or something similar to help you open an account. Find a search engine and type in "Poker Variations" and you'll score around 100,000 hits. There are a lot of people out there with an interest in the game.

LEFT
The picture illustrates the options available to you once you have successfully logged-in with poker variations, several other card games and gambling opportunities just a click away.

RIGHT
Under the Texas Hold 'Em tab, a list of available games is shown top left. The situation at the highlighted table, Alexandria, is indicated top right.

But what's it like to play poker via the internet? Well, the instant reaction to that question is to describe it as cool, fast, and exciting fun. Certainly when playing for real money, even if only small sums, the speed at which you must make decisions gives an appealing edge to proceedings. The various online poker rooms also offer no-risk "play-money" games that are fast and loose affairs. As you might expect, with no penalty for losing all your chips, pots are called to a showdown by many players, leaving little room for a successful bluff.

The astonishing growth in online poker is a twenty-first century phenomenon with the first online card room, ParadisePoker.com, opening for business just before the millennium. Now there are over 140 similar sites catering for poker players seeking a game to match their mood from the comfort of their own home. A 600 percent increase in business over the past year suggests that it is catching on in a big way. Interestingly, the convenience and, perhaps, the anonymity associated with playing online has led to women representing 40 percent of the card-room clientele, compared to just 5 percent in real-life card rooms and casinos. It's tempting to think that this signals another move toward poker becoming a respectable pastime.

So how does online poker work? Well, having selected the virtual casino at which you wish to play, you next have to register as a member. For the purposes of research, of course, I opened an account with PokerRoom.com, which is one of the more established sites and was recommended to me by a friend. As mentioned earlier, there are well over a 140 such sites offering online poker and other casino games. It is worth pointing out that not all states, countries, or cultures actually approve of gambling and some actively legislate against it. Indeed, many of the online casinos are based in countries with a relaxed attitude to the phenomenon. The best advice is to check out the ground rules first before becoming involved. After all, you don't want the Feds interrupting your game, especially when you're just about to win a big pot.

If you decide online poker is a good idea, you'll be required to create a username and a password to enable you to access the site of your choice. Bear in mind that the username you choose will be the "handle" by which you are identified at the table when you play. Unless you are prepared to make a deposit via credit card or something similar, you will not be able to access the real-money games. For a beginner this may be no bad thing, although playing for even a modest amount of money, will concentrate your thoughts far better than a play-money game.

RIGHT
By using the scroll bar to the right of the listed tables, it is possible to find a game for high-stakes play money if you wish. For beginners, this offers a chance to practice the game without losing.

BELOW
For some volatile action, there are even no-limit play money games on offer.

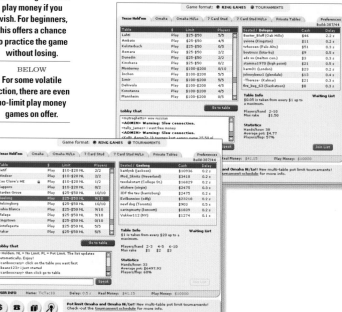

Provided you have registered without any problems, the site administrators will e-mail you notification that your account has been activated within a few minutes. Now you can play.

Once you've logged in, the window exhibiting the games available will load up and you'll probably be amazed at how many people are out there playing poker. The figure was over eight thousand on the first occasion I logged on and that's just one site. A tab for each poker variation exists and you should select the game with which you feel most comfortable—in my case, this is Texas Hold 'Em.

Having done that, a list of virtual tables is shown with indications of the stake level being applied, the betting structures in operation and, importantly, whether the game is for real money or not. The number of players, to a maximum of ten, is also indicated. Highlighting one of the tables that interests you will cause another window on screen to open up and list the names of the players currently sitting in on that game along with the size of their bankrolls. Double click on the highlighted table and a window will open offering a visual representation of the game in progress.

If you wish, you may simply watch the play for a while without participating in the game. This means that you can take a little time to assess your potential opposition and study their playing styles.

LEFT
Once at the table, click on an available seat ready to play. Then indicate how much money you wish to exchange for chips. Note the commentary box, bottom right, which records each action.

BELOW
The player is in the big blind and is dealt A 8 offsuit as the remainder ponder their betting moves.

185 ♥

The representative characters at the table, or caricatures to be more precise, are always the same, although it's best not to get too hung up about always being the old lady or the guy who looks like a pimp. Focus on the seating position and where you want to be in relation to the key players as indicated by their chip stack.

Once you highlight the seat and click on it, the information box in the corner of the screen will state that you are preparing to enter the game. All you have to do is select how much money you wish to convert into chips and then you are ready to click on the sit-in button and wait to be dealt a hand. From then on, the action is fast but quite straightforward. The player to bet is always highlighted as the action moves around the table and speech bubbles appear as the players fold, check, bet, or raise. When it is your turn to act, three buttons appear indicating that you can fold, check, or bet or, if a bet has already been made in the round, fold, call, or raise. Your hand is always visible face up and, as play progresses, folded hands disappear from the table. Your opponents' hands are represented by two cards face down in front of them and give you a quick visual clue as to who remains in each hand.

The action is fast and each player has only a limited time of around 15 seconds to make a betting decision. One of the reasons for this is that, in keeping with real casinos, the online casinos are taking a small percentage of each pot to cover the costs of the service. This is called "the rake" and the more games that are played, the more the casino earns for the services it provides.

Having spent a few hours playing online, I'd recommend that anybody considering doing so should be clear in their own mind about how long they intend to play at any one session. It is far too easy to keep seeing just one more hand and before you know it, there's another hour gone.

LEFT
Having checked on the flop with 10 7 offsuit, this player faces a tough decision on whether to gamble on an 8 for the gut-straight draw. It could be a winner, but a lot of players are betting. Should he fold, call, or raise?

Time, gentlemen please. If you want one more, come back tomorrow.

IS IT SAFE?

There are two aspects to this question, one of which concerns the integrity of the online casino operations, and one regarding the possibility of cheating and collusion. The first is easier to answer in that the business levels and the money involved have generated competition between companies offering the service. It is in their interests to make the financial dealings as simple but secure as possible. This includes a policy of offering you the chance to restrict your participation in games by means of responsible game settings. You can opt to exclude yourself from playing too often or for too much money if you feel there might be a problem. Breach your self-imposed conditions and the system will lock you out. The other question is much more difficult to answer. If there's a chance to operate a scam, somebody will have tried it. It is possible that a group of people could work together with sufficient computers to access the same game and tip the odds in their favor by sharing information. But if they do, it is bound to happen in one of the big money games to make it worthwhile and these games are likely to be more closely monitored by the company's security section for indications of fraudulent activity.

Of course, should you find that the competition at the table is too hot or simply not stimulating enough, you can leave at any time and rejoin the lobby area from where you can then access another table that is more to your liking. A feature of the lower stakes tables is that player turnover is very high, with seats being vacated and filled with surprising rapidity. Don't imagine that you'll be playing with the same half-dozen virtual players. The reality is that you could sit at the same table for an hour and compete against fifteen or twenty opponents. Some will have lost their chips and vacated a seat, others will be slipping off quickly having made a killing, either to bank their winnings or seek a higher-stakes game.

Should you be skillful enough to win, you can request that real money payments be made to the account you set up initially to pay your entry fee. So, the possibility exists to develop your game and also to clear a credit card debt at the same time, if you're good enough. It's a tantalizing prospect and one that seems destined to maintain the popularity of online poker for a while yet.

LEARNING FROM ONLINE POKER

The obvious benefit that online poker offers the novice player is the chance to practice. Without going to the trouble of finding a card room or organizing a game, you can still find yourself in the company of a few thousand like-minded souls eager for a game. The games available are the most popular: Texas Hold 'Em, Seven-Card Stud, Omaha, and the high-low split pot versions of the latter two. Focus on the variation you enjoy most and pick a table. The play-money games, although naturally very loose affairs, present you with an inexpensive way to learn the game and understand its ebbs and flows. When you feel confident in your play, then perhaps you're ready to start playing for real money.

BELOW
This example shows how a player's decision to check is indicated. In this case, it is after the flop.

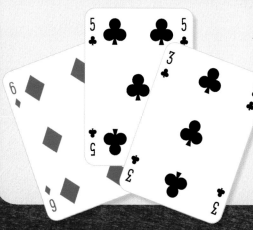

LEFT
As you can see,
the table is full as
the cards are dealt
and the blinds
automatically levied.
If you wish, you can
simply watch the
action for a while.

ABOVE
The pot stands at $77
in a subsequent hand
as the flop reveals a
pair of Qs. If you have
a Q in the hole, it
could be tricky to
extract more chips
from your opponents.
If you don't, it's just
plain tricky!

BELOW
If big money games are intimidating, the lower stakes fixed-limit games, such as this one, may be more appealing. Note, the two players to the right of the dealer button have just sat in and must make a compulsory bet equal to the big blind.

RIGHT
A customer's account balance details showing $45.05 in real money and $9,930 in play money. Avoid confusing the two.

BETTING DISCIPLINE

By now you will have gathered that poker is a gambling game that loses its meaning unless something valuable is at stake. If you are really serious about playing poker and want to continue to improve your play, then the few pointers in this section will help you. If you're not serious about the game, then you are either wealthy enough not to worry about it, or you're someone who resigns yourself to losing every time you take a seat at the table. Good luck to you both.

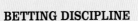

For the rest of us, improving our game means understanding what is happening at the table and counting our chips to see whether we are ahead or not. If you leave the table with more chips than you started on most occasions, you are probably a good player. However, unless you accurately record details of your poker betting, you will never know for sure just how good. Noting your betting behavior, whatever you're chosen gambling option, is the first step toward being objective about your style, your technique, and your strategy. Otherwise you should accept that you are a casual player. If that sounds like you, console yourself with the fact that it's not too late to change.

In poker, the chips are simply an indicator of success or failure in a game. When playing, this is how they should be regarded, which is why it is important to play at the stake level that enables you to do this. One guideline is to set aside a bankroll equivalent to 300 bets. If you play in a game where the maximum bet is $5, that works out as $1,500. Maybe that sounds like a lot, but reserving that level of cash enables you to play through spells when the statistically possible but highly improbable poker hands keep beating you.

STOCK ANSWERS
—◆—

Most casual gamblers, when asked how they are doing, will offer stock answers along the following lines:

Answer	*Meaning*
"I'm up."	"I think I'm slightly ahead."
"I'm about even."	"I might be slightly down."
"I'm doing OK."	"I'm well down."
"Not too good."	"I don't know when I'm next going to eat and the wife/girlfriend/boss/kids/mom/dad are going to kill me."

KEEPING A RECORD

Should you think of taking poker seriously, perhaps to semipro level, it's a good idea to start recording not just your ups and downs, but the rate at which you are winning—or losing—per hour. Say you are good enough to earn $20,000 a year from poker alone. That's great if you play once every three months, but what if you have to put in 80 hours a week? Suddenly the return on your time isn't so impressive, even if it might be a cool occupation.

Above all, bear in mind that once you are hooked on poker, you'll be playing it as often as you want for the rest of your life. So taking a long-term view will enable you to rationalize the occasional loss because it is unrealistic to expect to win every time. Quitting when ahead or quitting when behind during any particular session becomes incidental when you know you'll be back tomorrow, next week, or next month. Ultimately, it is important to be honest with yourself and to be realistic about your interest in the game.

ABOVE
Even the most successful players occasionally find compelling reasons for taking a break.

ABOVE
Affecting a call to elicit a response from an opponent and then raising is a sure way to render yourself unpopular.

POKER ETIQUETTE

Wherever you play poker, the following suggestions on how players should conduct themselves at the table are accepted as the norm. Each home game may have its own quirk idiosyncrasies, but this guide will help you to avoid making yourself look like a complete jerk.

First, always keep your cards and chips in full view of all other players and avoid touching anyone else's during play. Also, do not make a habit of showing your hand, during play or when folded, to one player. Any information is valuable at the poker table and this sort of behavior, however innocuous, smacks of favoritism. Remember, show one show all. Similarly, when discarding cards, take care not to expose them. If it happens, make sure everybody is aware what was exposed.

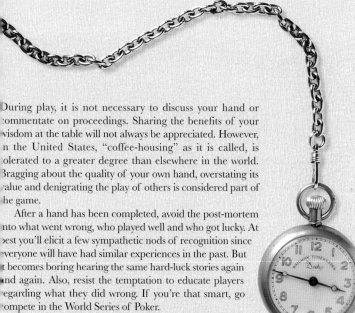

During play, it is not necessary to discuss your hand or commentate on proceedings. Sharing the benefits of your wisdom at the table will not always be appreciated. However, in the United States, "coffee-housing" as it is called, is tolerated to a greater degree than elsewhere in the world. Bragging about the quality of your own hand, overstating its value and denigrating the play of others is considered part of the game.

After a hand has been completed, avoid the post-mortem into what went wrong, who played well and who got lucky. At best you'll elicit a few sympathetic nods of recognition since everyone will have had similar experiences in the past. But it becomes boring hearing the same hard-luck stories again and again. Also, resist the temptation to educate players regarding what they did wrong. If you're that smart, go compete in the World Series of Poker.

If anyone needs help at the table, it may well be the dealer. If an error or miscalculation is made by the dealer during the game, then all players should be willing to speak up and point it out. That will benefit everybody.

Be clear in stating your betting intentions. Everyone at the table is seeking information to help them win a hand, so mumbled statements coupled with indeterminate actions are guaranteed to confuse players eager to find meaning in every gesture. If you intend to raise or bet all-in, say so and be quick about stating how much you are betting. Drawn-out betting moves to induce a reaction in opponents are known as "string bets" and will not be tolerated. Affecting a call and then diving back to your chip stack to make a raise when you see the next player pick up his chips for a bet will leave you friendless at the table. And poker is hard enough without that kind of handicap.

It follows from this that you should not take too long over a decision. Casinos opt for the two-minute rule, meaning that a player has two minutes to make a decision from the moment an opponent challenges them over the time they are taking.

Finally, don't try peeking at another player's cards. If they are so careless that you cannot help seeing them, discreetly point out their negligence when you have the chance. They may be complete beginners and not understand the significance of their mistake. But if you insist on trying to gather illicit information, one day you'll be caught out and invitations to play may well dry up.

ABOVE
Poker works best when players make prompt betting decisions. The "two-minute rule" helps to keep the game flowing.

SUMMARY

The expansion of interest in poker over the last thirty years or so has been given fresh impetus by the regular televising of the game and the opportunities available to play online from home. Armed with some of the ideas contained within this book, it is hoped that poker novices will be able to sample the poker experience, wherever they find it, without making fools of themselves or losing far more money than is good for their financial and spiritual health.

Perhaps the game is something you remember playing years ago but has long since disappeared from your social calendar. In that case, maybe this book has helped refresh your memory and revived your interest.

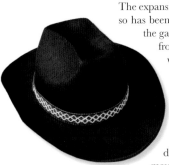

ABOVE
You may be a beginner, but once you've thrown your hat in the ring you could be the next poker pioneer to strike it rich.

Throughout, the aim has been to explain some of the basic concepts behind the most widely played poker variations in order to get you started. Having been played in one form or another for hundreds of years, poker doesn't seem in any hurry to go away. That means there is always a chance to enjoy the entertainment, intellectual challenges, and possibly even the financial rewards that come from playing the game.

For that to happen, a player must always be thinking about improving his or her skills. Experience at the table helps, but don't neglect the massive amount of information available in print and online that reflects the knowledge of countless poker experts.

Why anyone might want to play is going to be dictated by the nature of the individual concerned. Poker is a sociable pastime and can be enjoyed as such with a minimum of competitive urgency. If that is the level at which you are content to play, that's fine. It is essential to your enjoyment of the game that you set yourself a realistic target regarding exactly what you expect from poker. On the other hand, if you view yourself as a potential world champion, this book may represent merely the first small step on your way to acquiring the skills needed to succeed. Detailed theories on poker strategy and betting techniques will serve as good preparation as you head for your next game in search of practical experience.

Ultimately, you should approach poker in the same way as you approach so many other facets of life. If you work hard at the game and absorb lessons from your mistakes, then the likelihood is that your game will improve. And the better you begin to play, the more likely you are to win, which is, after all, the primary reason for playing. But poker can teach a player how to accept defeat and loss, too, encouraging them to come to terms with the fact that they alone are responsible for their decisions and actions.

Once discovered, the poker trail can lead you through hostile country, beautiful landscapes, and miles of barren desert. The journey will last a lifetime so keep moving on until you find the next watering hole. And then, who knows? It could just be time for another poker pioneer to strike it rich.

BELOW
Poker is a journey of discovery that you can enjoy until the end of time.

All aboard the poker express for the journey of a lifetime, folks!

GLOSSARY OF POKER TERMS

ACES UP Signifies two pair: As with another, lower, pair.

ACTION The betting activity around the poker table.

ALL-IN Staking all your chips in the pot with a single bet.

ANTE A compulsory bet made by players before the deal.

BACK-DOOR Hitting the flush with the last two board cards dealt in games like Hold 'Em and Omaha, usually when not expected.

BACK-DOOR STRAIGHT Same as above, except that the player completes an unlikely straight.

BAD BEAT When a good hand is beaten, against the odds, by someone drawing a better one.

BANKROLL Cash available to exchange for chips when sitting in a game. Your bankroll is simply your stake money.

BET To put money in the pot.

BETTING INTERVALS The occasions during the playing of the hand when betting rounds occur.

BICYCLE The lowest straight, comprising 5, 4, 3, 2, A. Also called a "wheel."

BIG SLICK Jargon for an A K as your hole cards in Texas Hold 'Em.

BLIND Compulsory bet made by the player immediately to the dealer's left. Usually, the first player to the left bets a small blind, and the next a big blind.

BLUFF An attempt to conceal the true value of your cards, usually by misrepresenting a weak hand with strong betting.

BOARD The set of community cards revealed on the table in Hold 'Em and Omaha, for example.

BOAT Slang term for a full house.

BUG A single wild card, typically the Joker.

BUMP To increase the betting level.

BURN The dealer's action of discarding the top card of the deck before the flop in community games to prevent cheating. The action should be repeated every time a further community card (fourth street, fifth street, etc.) is revealed.

BUY-IN The minimum fee for permission to sit in at a poker game.

CALL Matching a bet already made to continue playing the hand.

CARDS SPEAK The method of determining a winning hand from cards revealed at the showdown, without being subject to a declaration. Declarations are generally applied in high-low games.

CASH IN Exchanging chips for cash on leaving the game.

CHECK To defer an option to bet when the opportunity arises. A player can only check if no bet has yet been made during the betting round.

CHECKRAISE The act of checking and later raising an opponent's bet when the action comes back to you.

CHIPS Colored counters used to represent cash when playing poker. Different colors help distinguish between the cash denominations.

COMMUNITY Those cards that are revealed on the table and are common to all players.

CRYING CALL A call made when a player does not believe they will win.

CUT The action of dividing the deck after the dealer has shuffled, usually the responsibility of the player to the dealer's right.

DEALER'S CHOICE An agreement to allow the dealer to name the game to be played. As the deal moves around the table, so the prospect of many variations being played arises, making it popular in some games.

DECLARE In high-low games, the decision taken by players to aim for the high hand, low hand, or both.

DEUCE Slang for any 2 in the deck.

DRAW The exchange of cards during a poker game.

DRAWING DEAD The situation of being unable to beat an existing hand while still having cards to come. Definitely not good.

FAMILY POT A pot involving most if not all the players at the table.

FIFTH STREET Generic term for the fifth card dealt in poker games. These are punctuated by betting intervals, like Hold 'Em and Omaha, for example. As the fifth card is also the last community card dealt in these two games, it is sometimes called "the river."

FISH A poor player.

FIXED LIMIT Betting that is structured, with maximum stake levels applying throughout the game. In Draw Poker, for example, bets and raises of $5 may apply for the first round. After the draw, the second round betting limit might be increased to $10, making it a $5/$10 game.

FLOORMAN The arbitrator of disputes and the general authority on the rules in a card room.

FLOP The first three community cards revealed in the relevant poker variation.

FLUSH A five-card hand that contains cards of the same suit but not in any sequential order.

FOLD To discard one's hand.

FORCED BET A bet made at a fixed amount.

FOURTH STREET The fourth card dealt in games punctuated by betting intervals. In Hold 'Em and Omaha, it is also called the "turn."

FREE CARD A card received by players without having to bet beforehand, for example, if everybody checks during a betting round.

FREEZE-OUT Tournament-related term indicating that players start with an equal amount of chips and are eliminated, one by one, when they have exhausted their stack.

FULL HOUSE Three cards of one rank and two of another.

GUT STRAIGHT DRAW Holding cards such as 8, 9, J, Q and needing the "middle Draw pin" to make a straight.

HAND The term describing the cards each player uses during the game. Also used to describe each individual game dealt during a session.

HEADS UP Playing against just one other opponent.

HOLE (CARDS) Cards dealt to you face down at the start of a hand that are unknown to opponents are said to be "in the hole." Also known as "pocket cards."

INSIDE STRAIGHT DRAW Similar to a gut straight, but it's the other cards that are required. For example A, Q, J, 10 or 9, 8, 7, 5.

KICKER The highest retained card aside from a stronger holding. For example A, A, K, 9, 6 is a pair of Aces with a King kicker.

KITTY The pot of chips for each hand contested.

LOOSE PLAYER Someone who regularly bets against the odds.

MAIN POT The original pot up to the point when a player goes all-in. Other players remaining in the hand may then bet against each other into a side pot.

MANIAC A very loose player.

MISDEAL Describes an error made in dealing a hand.

MUCK Colorful expression for the pile of discarded cards. It also describes the act of folding, in other words, "mucking the hand."

NO-LIMIT A no-limit game enables players to bet as much as they wish whenever it is their turn to act. Usually seen in tournament play.

NUTS The best available hand from the cards played.

OFFSUIT Used to describe cards that do not match suits, usually in Hold 'Em.

OPEN-ENDED STRAIGHT hand with four cards in consecutive order that can make a straight with a card on either end. For example, J, 10, 9, 8 where a 7 or Q will make the hand. The Q obviously gives you the "high-end" draw, while the 7 puts you at the low, or "ignorant," end of the hand.

OPENERS Cards required in the hand to start the betting. Traditionally, a pair of Js or better are be the openers required to bet in Draw Poker.

PASS An alternative way of saying "fold."

PAT HAND A hand in Draw Poker that is dealt to a player who declines to draw further cards when given the chance. It usually means it cannot be improved on, though players are known to bluff in this situation.

POCKET PAIR Two cards of the same rank dealt to you during Texas Hold 'Em.

POCKET ROCKETS Two As dealt to you during Texas Hold 'Em.

POKER FACE An expressionless facial appearance revealing no thoughts or emotions. Every player should have one.

POT The chips staked for each individual hand.

POT-LIMIT A game in which the maximum bet can be no higher than the amount already in the pot.

QUADS Four of a kind.

RAG A worthless card or hand.

RAISE To call a bet and then stake additional chips to raise the betting. Usually, a raise must be equal to the value of the previous bet. So, if the previous player bet $5, you can expect to stake a minimum $10 when raising—$5 to call the previous bet and $5 to raise. Be clear in announcing an intention to raise. A raise can be less than the required minimum when a player announces "all-in."

RAISER The player who makes the raise.

READ The act of determining the quality of hand a player holds from the information available to you.

RIVER The final community card dealt in relevant poker games.

ROCK A tight or conservative player who plays only premium hands.

ROYAL FLUSH The highest hand in poker—A, K, Q, J, 10 of the same suit.

RUN Another term for a straight.

RUSH Experienced when a player is on a hot winning streak.

SANDBAG To slow play a hand.

SEE To call a bet.

SEMI-BLUFF A bet made on a hand that may not be the best, but has chances of improving past an opponent's hand.

SHOWDOWN The moment when the cards are revealed to determine the winner.

SIDE POT Chips bet by players competing separately from the main pot, usually after another player has bet all-in.

SLOW PLAY Betting lightly, or checking, to disguise the strength of a hand in an attempt to encourage more players to stay in the pot.

SPLIT POT A pot shared between players who have the same value hand at the showdown. Also used to describe games in which the pot is split between the best high and low hands, like Omaha/8.

SPREAD LIMIT Betting structured with a lower and upper limit, for example $1–$5. Bets and raises may be made for any amount during the game within these limits.

STRAIGHT Five unsuited cards in sequential order. Also called a run.

STRAIGHT FLUSH Five suited cards in sequential order.

STRING BET An illegal betting move in which a player calls a bet and then, without announcing "raise," bets more chips from his stack.

SUCKER A very poor player.

TABLE STAKES A game in which players are limited to playing with only the stakes they bring to the table. Pot-limit and no-limit games are good examples.

TAP OUT To bet all one's chips.

TAPPED OUT Out of chips and in Tap City!

TELL A mannerism, usually involuntary, that can indicate the strength of a player's hand.

TIGHT PLAYER Somebody who bets very cautiously and only on strong hands.

TILT A word to describe playing wildly and without discipline, usually after experiencing a series of bad beats.

TOKE A tip for the card room dealer.

TREY Any 3.

TRIPS Three of a kind, short for triplets.

TURN CARD The fourth common card dealt in Texas Hold 'Em and Omaha, also referred to as "fourth street."

UNDERDOG The hand that is unlikely to be the winner, often called "dog" for short.

WHEEL The lowest straight, comprising 5, 4, 3, 2, A. Also called a "bicycle."

WILD CARD A card or cards that, having been agreed upon by the players, may count as any card in the pack. If deuces are wild, then all the 2s in the pack can be counted as whatever value card you wish.

RECOMMENDED WEBSITES

The sites listed below represent a mere handful of the vast array of poker and poker-related internet domains that exist to serve those interested in the game. Type "Poker Variations" into your search engine and you will register around 100,000 hits, giving you some idea of poker's popularity around the world.

www.casinocity.com

A site with all the latest news and developments on the gambling scene, both in the United States and the rest of the world.

www.rec.gambling.poker

A global newsroom in which poker nuts can find out all they need to know about the latest developments in the game, as well as exchange information with each other.

www.homepoker.com
www.ildado.com/uk_cardroom_guide.html
www.pagat.com
www.poker.net
www.pokertop10.com
www.pokermike.com
www.playwinningpoker.com
www.pokertips.org
www.pokernews.info
www.cardgamerules.homestead.com
www.goodgamblingguide.co.uk

All of these sites have a wealth of poker information for both the beginner and the regular player. Not only do they possess sections on how to play the hundreds of variations that exist, but they also offer news from the poker world and reviews of tournament play. For the serious poker fan, there is plenty of advice and guidance available regarding strategy, probability theory, and statistical analysis to help improve your skills in a range of games.

RECOMMENDED BOOKS

H ere is a small selection from the numerous books about poker that will help the novice player learn more about the game. Some are recommended because of their technical detail, including advice on how to play the popular variations to a respectable level. Others are more biographical or anecdotal in nature, offering entertaining insights into the world of regular card games and the lives of full-time, professional poker players.

The Biggest Game in Town by AL ALVAREZ (Boston: Houghton Mifflin, 1983) is an entertaining and lively account of the 1981 World Series of Poker, which paints a vivid picture of poker players in general and Las Vegas in particular.

Poker Nation by ANDY BELLIN (London: Yellow Jersey Press, 2000) is part guidebook, part autobiography, with each chapter colorfully explaining technical aspects of poker using examples drawn from Bellin's own experiences as a semi-professional.

Thursday-Night Poker: How to Understand, Enjoy and Win by PETER O. STEINER (New York: Random House, 1996) is a thorough and searching examination of poker approached with academic zeal. This book explains all aspects of the game before applying the lessons to the most popular variations.

The Rules of Neighborhood Poker According to Hoyle by STEWART WOLPIN (New York: New Chapter Press, 1990) covers the world of home poker games in a breezy style with guidelines on how to play around forty variations.

Super System: A Course in Poker Power by DOYLE BRUNSON (Las Vegas: B & G Publishing, 1978) represents the thoughts of a two-time World Series of Poker champion.

The Theory of Poker (formerly called *Winning Poker*) by DAVID SKLANSKY (Two Plus Two Publishing, 1992) is acknowledged as a classic of its kind. The same author is also responsible for *Hold 'Em Poker* (Two Plus Two Publishing, 1996), a guide to playing Texas Hold 'Em for high stakes. And for those who want to develop their Omaha skills, *Omaha Hold 'Em Poker* by BOB CIAFFONE (Las Vegas: Harris Printers, 1992) is a brief but thorough guide to the high-only version of the game.

These represent just a few suggestions from the ever-expanding realm of literature relating to poker. If you simply enjoy playing for fun, there are plenty of biographical books that can transport you to a tournament's final table to relive the experience of a world champion, albeit from a distance. Alternatively, there are many others that will broaden the knowledge and expertise of aspiring players and would-be professionals.

And since successful poker demands patience, observation, and a willingness to learn, any opportunity to consider another player's experience is always well worth taking.

INDEX

ACKNOWLEDGMENTS

AUTHOR'S ACKNOWLEDGMENTS

In writing this beginner's guide to Poker I have, of course, called upon the help and assistance of a number of generous people, not all of whom are avid poker players. Particular thanks go to Sophie Collins, Jason Hook, and Rebecca Saraceno at The Ivy Press Ltd for their faith and encouragement, and I must extend my gratitude to Alison Jenkins for introducing me to the publishers.

Simon Garwood offered a helping hand in guiding me towards the pleasures of online poker and I also owe many thanks to the guys at www.pokerroom.com for their assistance. Finally, I'd like to extend my appreciation to the various poker players who have invited me to risk my money in the comfort of their homes. So thank you Russell, Pete H, Rupert, Pete G, Stewart, Steve P, Al, Tom, Ian, Jude, Julian, Tracy, Steve G, Mack, Brendan, Justin, Alistair S, Alastair Mac, Paul R, Mike, and Paul S. Finally, I am compelled to thank the lovely Gosia Pilak for her patience and understanding throughout the weeks it took to write the book. Dziekuje, kochanie.

PICTURE ACKNOWLEDGMENTS

The publishers would like to thank the following for the use of pictures. Every effort has been made to trace copyright holders and obtain permissions. The publishers apologize for any omissions, and would be pleased to make any necessary changes for subsequent printings.

☆ **The United States Playing Card Company:** BICYCLE, the BICYCLE Ace of Spades design, the BICYCLE Rider Back design and all other brand elements are registered trademarks of The United States Playing Card Company in the United States and other countries, used on the cover with permission from The United States Playing Card Company.

☆ **www.richard-edward.com.** Many thanks for supplying cards for use inside the book.

☆ **Library of Congress, Prints and Photographs Division:** pp. 7, 8, 13, 154, 177, 196.

☆ **Corbis:** pp. 11 +161 +167 Bureau L.A. Collection, 14 John Springer Collection, 19 Hulton-Deutsch Collection, 34 + 116 John Springer Collection, 137 + 164/5 Bettmann Archive.

☆ **Films:** Annie Get Your Gun/courtesy RKO: pp. 27, 68. Arizona/courtesy Columbia Pictures: p. 116. Calamity Jane/courtesy Warner Bros.: pp. 48, 52, 111. Cheyenne Autumn/courtesy Warner Bros.: pp. 3, 99. Destry Rides Again/courtesy Universal: p. 193. Goodfellas/courtesy Warner Bros.: p. 144. Gone With the Wind/courtesy MGM: p. 170. Hearts of the West/courtesy United Artists: p.172. Heart of the Man/courtesy Rank: p. 180. Irma la Douce/courtesy United Artists: p. 163. Jesse James versus the Daltons/courtesy Columbia Pictures: pp. 41, 51, 178. The Sons of Katie Elder/courtesy Paramount: p. 42. Maverick/courtesy Icon Productions: pp. 11, 161, 167. Nevada Smith/courtesy Joseph E Levine/ Paramount: p. 36. Old Oklahoma Plains/courtesy Republic Pictures International inc.: pp. 85, 174. Pale Rider/courtesy Warner Bros. p. 96. Stagecoach/courtesy 20th Century Fox: p. 187. The Apartment/courtesy United Artists: pp. 22. The Cincinnati Kid/courtesy MGM/Filmways: pp. 112, 139. The Odd Couple/ courtesy Paramount: p. 34. The Sting/courtesy Universal: p. 148. Tombstone/courtesy Hollywood Pictures/CINERGI: pp. 28, 62. West of Carson City: p.14. Wild Bill/courtesy United Artists: pp. 10, 33, 46. Your Cheatin Heart/courtesy MGM: p. 179.

☆ **www.pokerroom.com:** 150–151, 182–191.